21 Things

Every Home

Inspector

Should Know

Practical Advice for Building a
Successful Home Inspection Career

Frank Cook

Pat Remick

Dearborn
Home Inspection
Education

This publication is designed to provide accurate and authoritative information in regard to the subject matter covered. It is sold with the understanding that the publisher is not engaged in rendering legal, accounting, or other professional service. If legal advice or other expert assistance is required, the services of a competent professional person should be sought.

President: Roy Lipner
Vice-President of Product Development and Publishing: Evan Butterfield
Associate Publisher: Louise Benzer
Senior Development Editor: Tony Peregrin
Managing Editor, Production: Daniel Frey
Quality Assurance Editor: David Shaw
Typesetter: Janet Schroeder
Creative Director: Lucy Jenkins

Published by Dearborn™ Real Estate Education,
a division of Dearborn Financial Publishing, Inc.®
30 South Wacker Drive
Chicago, IL 60606-7481
(312) 836-4400
www.dearbornRE.com

Printed in the United States of America
05   06   07   10   9   8   7   6   5   4   3   2   1

Library of Congress Cataloging—in—Publication Data

Cook, Frank (Frank T.), 1948–
   21 things every home inspector should know / Frank Cook and Pat Remick.— 1st ed.
      p. cm.
   Includes index.
   ISBN 0-7931-9623-X
   1. Dwellings—Inspection. I. Title: Twenty-one things every home inspector should know. II. Remick, Pat. III. Title.

TH4817.5.C66 2005
643'.12—dc22   2005003651

To our sons, J.D. and Dan, who forever will be our greatest works
and inspiration; and to our mothers, Marion and Pat, who
allowed us to dream that one day a love of writing might actually
earn a paycheck.

P r e f a c e   ix

A c k n o w l e d g m e n t s   xiii

C h a p t e r 1

Come On In and Join Us!   1

Um, did anyone mention the fine print on the back of the invitation?

C h a p t e r 2

How Did You Get in Here?   9

Do you have what it takes to be a home inspector?

C h a p t e r 3

What Do You Need to Know?   19

And where can you go to learn it?

C h a p t e r 4

Home Inspection: It Isn't Just a Man's World   31

There's no reason why women can't succeed, and thrive, in this business.

C h a p t e r 5

Tools of the Trade   37

Let's talk start-up costs.

C h a p t e r 6

Market Thyself   45

You may be a great home inspector, but nobody will know it unless you sell yourself.

C h a p t e r 7

Where Do You Fit in the Deal?   65

What happened before you got to the house and what's going to happen after you leave?

C h a p t e r 8

Who Is Your Client?   81

The guy who writes me a check! Right? (That *is* right, isn't it?)

C h a p t e r 9

Getting Paid   89

You can make $100,000 your first year, but you may not pocket enough to live on.

C h a p t e r 1 0

How Busy Can You Be? It Depends.   97

The realities of endless possibilities...

C h a p t e r 1 1

How Far Does the Inspection Have to Go?   103

Are you going to be able to restrict your inspection to just the home, or will it go into the yard and down the street?

C h a p t e r 1 2

How Dangerous Is This Job?   109

Imagine what you'd look like standing naked on someone's roof.

Chapter 13

Working with Buyers 115

Patience is the queen of all virtues—and nowhere is that truer than in the home inspection business.

Chapter 14

Getting Along Without You 123

Should you defend against the do-it-yourselfer?

Chapter 15

Liability and the Courts 129

Lawyers did not create the home inspection business, but they were there at the birth.

Chapter 16

Everything Is About Ethics 139

Why it is important not to lie to your client, and to be careful about who you take money from.

Chapter 17

The Organizational You 147

Sometimes you wanna go where everybody knows your name.

Chapter 18

You're Involved in Politics 161

Whether you want to be or not, legislatures across the land are tinkering with your business.

Chapter 19

The Challenges Ahead 169

The real estate business already has survived (more or less) mold and asbestos. But you can be sure there are more challenges coming.

Chapter 20

What Else Can You Do?   177

With all the skills you have, all you need is a little imagination to come up with a raft of different ways to serve the marketplace.

Chapter 21

The High-Tech Home of the ...   185

Well, actually, the home of the future is already here.

Chapter 22

Why Do People Fail?   191

Every year a large number of people go into this business, and a large number are forced out. Why?

Chapter 23

In Conclusion...   197

Home inspecting can be both enjoyable and lucrative. You'll like it here.

Glossary   201

Index   213

Y ou've made the right decision in buying this book.
Certainly, we (the authors) appreciate your support, but
that's not why you are to be congratulated. You are to be congratulated because buying this book signals your intent to learn more
about the home inspection business before you jump in with
both feet (and your wallet).

This is not one of those "how to succeed" books, and it certainly isn't one of those "success guru" books. What we hope to
do here is point out some of the upsides—and downsides—of being
a home inspector. Our desired result is that when you reach the
end of this book, you'll say one of two things: either "Boy, I can
hardly wait to get started!" or "Geez, what was I thinking?!"

Ironically, those already making a career out of the inspection
business would equally applaud either decision on your part.

If you decide this is what you want to do with your life, you'll
be welcomed in. Alternatively, if you decide to stay out, you'll be
equally appreciated. Coming to the realization early that home
inspecting isn't for you is one of the best things you can do for
yourself—and the profession. Being a home inspector is one of
those jobs where you either fit or you don't. There's not a lot of
gray area, and it normally doesn't take very long to figure out
whether you belong.

As the editors of *Real Estate Intelligence Report*, in the years
we've been doing news coverage of the broader real estate industry from both a consumer's and a professional's point of view,
what we've found are three immutable truths about home
inspecting:

1. Knowing how a house works is one thing, but knowing how people work is another.
2. It doesn't matter who you think you are, the homebuyer thinks you're his or her hero.
3. If you're in the home inspection business, you're in politics. Get used to it.

The practice of home inspection, of course, is probably as old as the practice of living in homes. It's not too hard to imagine the earliest fatherly caveman visiting a cave selected by his daughter and future son-in-law, grunting a few times at the water seepage in the back, the lack of ventilation for the fire, and by the way, did they notice this cave was located on the side of a volcano?

Throughout the ages fathers, fathers-in-law, uncles, and close family friends have been asked to "check out" the homes of children starting out, just to make sure the houses were safe and sound and, of course, worth the money they were putting into it. The grudgingly offered verdict, "It'll do," was generally considered high praise indeed.

In the post–World War II era, however, as children began leaving home for distant places, families began spreading from coast to coast and the availability of a knowledgeable relative to walk through a home became much rarer. In many ways, the surrogate for that dad, in-law, or close friend became the home inspector.

(As you go forward in your career, it might do you well to remember who exactly you're standing in for. In the years ahead, your loyalty and your instincts are going to be challenged by other "professionals" whose vested interests will vary from those of your client. You will need to have a strong sense of where your loyalties lie.)

Today, most people date the modern home inspection business to the early 1970s—not really that long ago—when more homes were being built, more homes were being bought, and more people were becoming concerned about the conditions of the homes they were buying.

They wanted to put a bedroom in the basement. Did the basement leak?

The kitchen floor seemed uneven. Was there a problem?

Should they be worried about that spot on the ceiling?

What was that dirt tunnel going up the foundation?

And, not coincidentally, if the individual they consulted was wrong about the basement, the floor, the ceiling, or the termites, the consumer was prepared to go to court to find out why.

Clearly by the mid-1970s, it was time to set professional standards and train people who wanted to be in this business. From those needs arose the American Society of Home Inspectors®, and later the National Association of Home Inspectors, among others. Franchises began bringing modern business practices to the industry, and soon states like Texas and North Carolina began seeing the need to license and regulate the business on behalf of the consumer. That trend would quickly spread to other states as well. Yet, in the midst of all this organization, home inspectors themselves have continued to remain fiercely independent individuals. As mentioned above, the willingness to stand up to real estate agents, lawyers, and bankers is not a trait to be overlooked.

As you read on, you'll see that successful inspectors have come from a variety of walks of life. "Home inspector" rarely seems to be the first choice of a career for anyone, yet many of the nation's top inspectors today can't imagine being in any other business.

In the years ahead, perhaps you'll join those ranks of top professionals. Perhaps you won't. Either way, what you'll learn and experience in your first few weeks and months will stay with you for the rest of your life.

The purpose of this book is to shine a little light on the path you are about to take. But make no mistake—like most other professions, the road we'll travel is hardly the only one to the top.

Invariably, you will do much of the trailblazing yourself.

Feel free to break the mold. Feel free to innovate. There definitely is room for you in this business.

One final note: This book is not an original Shakespeare manuscript to be read once and then delicately placed back on a shelf. This is a working book. You should feel free to mark up sections you find important, write notes in the margins, and even dog-ear pages that you want to find later.

This book is no more fragile than any other tools in your toolbox. We hope you'll use it that way.

No book can be written by itself, and this one is no exception. In addition to the many individual professionals we've quoted here who contributed their time and insights to help increase the professionalism of their industry, there are others whose contributions should be noted.

We would especially like to thank three home inspector organizations whose members were especially generous with their knowledge and thoughts, and whose directors and media people helped us find some great interviews—The American Society of Home Inspectors and Jason Bird, Mallory Anderson and the National Association of Home Inspectors, and Nick Gromicko and the National Association of Certified Home Inspectors. Add to those Elizabeth Roane of AmeriSpec.

We also appreciate the foresight offered by the National Association of REALTORS® and the National Association of Home Builders.

Many individual inspectors helped guide the words in this book, and graciously contributed their expertise and observations. Among our most patient contributing sources were inspectors Skip Kelly, Mike Casey, John Merritt, Jamison Brown, Don Norman, Stephen Gladstone, and Alan Carson. Dennis Robitaille, Jay Schnoor, Ralph Wirth, Bill Mason, Stan Garnet, Frank Poliferno, and Troy Bloxom provided great perspectives. And thanks to the inspectors blazing trails in this industry who so generously shared their experiences: Diane Marotz, Michele Teague, Janice Ruhs, Mardi Clissold, Alyssa Hickson, Kimberly St. Louis, Lynette Gebben, and Shelly Barroner.

As always, our good friend Bill French helped provide balance and perspective.

Finally, we'd like to thank Dearborn Publishing and, in particular, Evan Butterfield and Tony Peregrin for their gentle reminders about deadlines and production schedules. Without them, this book would not be in your hands today.

CHAPTER 1

Come On In and Join Us

Um, did anyone mention the fine print on the back of the invitation?

Imagine yourself in a darkened conference room with 10 or 12 other people seated around you, all of you trying to decide if you want to go into the home inspection business. At the head of the table is a man in a suit doing a PowerPoint presentation. There is a bright white screen behind him and the computerized projector in front.

He's holding a remote control in his hand as he offers a few welcoming remarks. He passes out pieces of paper and invites you to follow along as he goes through his presentation. He begins his slide show:

Click.

Cover Slide: Deep blue screen with bright gold letters: "So You Want To Be a Home Inspector?"

Click.

Slide One: A chart appears. There are numbers going up the left side and stretched out along the bottom are a series of years, starting around 1960. On the graph itself is a bright red line, jagged, but generally sloping up at about a 45-degree angle. That, the speaker tells you, is the increasing number of people who are getting into the home inspection business every year.

Click.

Slide Two is the same as Slide One, except that now the speaker has superimposed a jagged blue line alongside the red one, and it too is going up roughly at a 45-degree angle. The blue depicts the percentage increase in the number of homes being inspected every year.

Click.

Again the same graph, but a bright green line has been added. It's a relatively flat line with a far more gradual rate of ascent. The green line is the average fee charged for home inspections across the country. Not a very rapid increase.

Click.

Slide Four. A black line that doesn't appear until about 1990, then shoots up. The amount of litigation against home inspectors.

Click.

Now a bright yellow line, staying pretty flat for several years but suddenly shooting upward, beginning about 1995. Technology finds its way into the home inspection business.

Click.

Another line. The amount of regulation being passed in state after state.

Click.

The amount of hours of training needed to get licensed.

Click.

Business startup costs.

Click.

Insurance.

Click.

Background education.

Click.

The presenter's remarks soon become irrelevant. The lines have taken over the story. Everything is higher, everything is more, everything is bigger, faster, more expensive, more efficient, harder to get, harder to do, and harder to understand.

Finally he turns off the projector and the lights come up in the room.

"Welcome," he says, "to the home inspection business of the new millennium."

The name of this book is *21 Things Every Home Inspector Should Know,* and basically it is for people who are either new to the business or still thinking about getting into it.

But before we go too deeply into the "21 Things," you'd be wise to reexamine the imaginary seminar you just attended above. As veterans of the industry will tell you, there are many remarkable things about what you just sat through, and you didn't even know it.

First and foremost, the speaker was a professional trainer wearing a suit, the session was held in a conference room, he was using technology to make his point, and there were a dozen or so people sitting there to hear what he had to say.

Not so very long ago, that meeting would have had an entirely different look and feel.

The "speaker," if you could call him that, would have been wearing coveralls, and instead of being in a conference room, he might have been leaning against his pickup truck. There wouldn't have been 10 or 12 people gathered around. There would have been you, and maybe someone else. And certainly all of you would have been men.

Instead of a PowerPoint show, his communication technology would have been a clipboard on the front seat of his pickup. If he wanted to change a chart, he would have used a pencil with an eraser.

Finally, there wouldn't have been any point-after-point and jagged-line-after-jagged line. Most of the ideas for those lines didn't even exist until the mid-1980s.

In the last 30 years or so, the home inspection business has gone from being a semiprofitable part-time job to being a full-blown, full-time, full-salary profession. And it is still growing and changing.

However, at this writing,

- fees charged have not caught up with liability incurred by inspectors, but . . .
- skills at hand also are lagging behind the skills expected by consumers.

- The vast majority of inspectors are using written contracts, but . . .
- the courts also are rewriting those contracts after the fact.

And more and more, real estate brokers, bankers, lawyers, and appraisers—and, of course, consumers—are looking at you as the professional in the deal. Unfortunately, the other side of "respect" is "liability." Not only are they *expecting* you to know what's going on with a house, they also are *depending* on you to know.

As you go through the following chapters, we's like you to remember that "21 Things" is a minimum, not a maximum. And it's a flexible minimum at that. Other authors and experts could easily come up with a different list—and yes, we urge you to explore those lists as well.

The "21 Things" we go through here also should not be an intimidating list. Odds are good that you already possess many of the skills needed by home inspectors, and the skills you don't have, you most likely will be able to pick up as you go along.

Think of it like this: On your first day on the job, you should know how to inspect a house; but it could be years before you really understand how the home inspection business works.

The good news, of course, is that there is every reason for you to have a positive attitude about your chances for success in this business, if for no other reason than that the industry itself really needs you to succeed. There has never been more demand for quality people in the inspection business, and every day the professional inspection organizations are working to put more tools in your hands (and in your head) to help you be successful.

Having said that, however, you also need to be prepared to be disappointed. There are things on this "21 Things" list that you may never have if you don't have them now. Some flaws are hard to work around.

So what is our version of the *21 Things Every Home Inspector Should Know?* As you read on you'll meet them in depth, but here they are in capsule form. Some are practical, some are philosophical, but we feel all of them will come into play if you are to have a successful career.

Don Norman, a long-time home inspector from St. Louis, puts it bluntly:

"If I had two candidates for the job, one with great technical skills but no people skills; the other with great people skills but few technical skills, I'd hire the one with fewer technical skills. I can teach technical skills," he says. ■

Here goes:

1. Who are the people who make up this industry and where did they come from? And what is their background?

2. There are certain minimum skills you need before you step into a house. If you don't have a basic understanding of electrical wiring, foundations, roofing systems, and plumbing, heating, and air-conditioning systems, then you could easily be a danger to yourself and others.

3. Despite what some people may believe, there is no reason why women can't move into the home inspection business and be just as successful as men. Already there are more women real estate agents than men (55 percent compared with 45 percent, according to the National Association of REALTORS®). Whom do you think those female real estate agents would like to refer business to?

4. You need to understand there are a certain number of tools you need—and some of them are expensive—before you take your first assignment. And new high-tech tools are on the way. You are going to be laying out a lot of money before you see a dime back. And by the way, don't forget about the costs of professional insurance, called *errors and omissions insurance* (or "E&O" insurance), and any business-related legal fees. You may be surprised at the number of times you may have to consult with an attorney for everything from incorporating your business to assessing your legal obligations to anyone you hire to work for you.

5. You need to know where your business is going to come from. Are you any good at marketing yourself? Do you even know who to market to? Do you know how to talk to consumers who don't believe they need a home inspection or, worse, think they can do it themselves?

6. You need to understand exactly where you fit in the real estate transaction. What's gone on before the buyer hired you? What happens after you hand over your report? Who are all the people involved in this business?

7. You need to understand who your client is (and who your client isn't) and how beholden you are to that client and to the other people in the transaction. You are going to be faced with "loyalty choices" and "good for business choices." Sometimes it's going to be a tough call.

8. Do you know how much to charge? Do you even know how to come up with a rate for your time and expertise?

9. How busy can you be? How many houses can you inspect and how much money can you make?

10. You need to make sure your client understands what you can do and what you can't do—and even what you *won't* do. What your client is really paying for is your ability to see the home's future. (And it would be helpful if you could see through walls, too.)

11. Probably every inspection you ever do has some element of risk. Do you have to climb on the roof or stick your hand into that dark hole in the basement?

12. It is important to bring homebuyers, especially first-time homebuyers, along on the inspection. But you also have to keep them out of trouble.

13. In some ways you are going to have to compete with a new phenomenon: the do-it-yourself home inspectors, who won't pay $400 to professionally inspect their new $400,000 home. Go figure.

14. You should understand that in many ways, the modern home inspection business has sprung from court rulings regarding liability. And the courts will continue to shape your life into the future.

15. Because you are so pivotal to the real estate transaction, people with a vested interest in your report are going to be watching you very closely. This is the time to keep your ethics close to you.

16. An important benefit to being a home inspector is that there are excellent support groups available to you. It is important to join the club, even it if costs you money.

17. Do you understand that if you are a home inspector, you are involved in politics—whether you want to be or not? Some states are licensing inspectors, others aren't. Now that you're here, you can help elevate the standards.

18. Do you know the challenges ahead? You're already aware of the potential problems from lead-based paint, formaldehyde, electromagnetic fields, radon, and mold—but what's next? Healthy houses, zero-energy homes?

19. Have you thought through what else you can do with your skills? If you think all you can do is inspect a house for a buyer, you have sold yourself way short.

20. Houses are changing, and so are the appliances in them. Do you need to know the latest performance specs every time GE comes out with a new dishwasher or water heater? Do you understand the complexities of computerized homes?

21. Do you know why people don't make it? Every year a certain number of people become home inspectors, and every year a certain number wash out. Why?

As we go forward from here, there are a couple of things we'd like you to keep close: A sense of perspective, and a sense of humor.

Not every issue is a big issue. Not every problem is a big problem.

As you go through your career, you are going to be confronted with things you've never seen before and never expected. The best advice? When you get into a jam, ask someone. Ask another inspector in town, someone you trust. Go to one of the national organizations and see if they have an answer. Join an online forum.

You are going to find that most of your peers in this business are happy to share what they know, will talk about best practices, and will stand behind you on ethical issues. The reputation of the entire industry is at stake. Now it's your turn to be part of that reputation.

Let's get started.

CHAPTER 2

How Did You Get in Here?

Do you have what it takes to be a home inspector?

If you're reading this book, you're already way ahead in the home inspection game.

The mere fact that you're reading these pages indicates you don't consider yourself an expert. You don't believe you can simply pick up a clipboard and a flashlight to get started. That realization can be a tremendous plus. It shows you are willing to learn, and that will be very important in the days ahead.

You may already have an inkling that the home inspection business might be complicated and require some expertise, and that you probably will need to continue educating yourself if you want to continue to succeed. But if you don't already have that inkling, or you picked up this book purely out of curiosity, that's OK, too. We're here to help you explore the possibilities and get an idea of the minimum you will need to know to get started in this business, without harming yourself or anyone else.

A hint here: Prior experience in the construction industry is not a requirement for success. Home inspection is evolving rapidly beyond the days when a guy in dirty coveralls would arrive in a pickup truck between stops at construction sites to poke around a house for a while, mumble a few things, and then hand over a scrap of paper with a few notes scribbled on it.

Today's computer-sophisticated homebuyers expect a professional appearance, a professional inspection, and a professional report (and don't much care whether their inspector is male or female).

The key word is *professional*. And how you get there is what this book is about.

Before the Beginning

You wouldn't start on a long trip unless you had two things: A map, and enough money to get you there safely. The same is true in business—any business.

The map, in this case, is a business plan where you set out in black ink on white paper exactly what you want to accomplish and how you are going to accomplish it. We talk more later about business plans, but basically you are going to write down how much money you need, where you are going to get it, how you are going to spend it, how much you realistically can expect in return for your first year, and what you are going to live on while waiting for that return. In a sense, much of this book can be seen as your map.

Obviously, you don't want to leap into the home inspection business unless you have some money (and by "some money" we actually mean "a lot of money") stashed away to hold you over until your income starts catching up to your outflow. Specifically: You need to have enough money stockpiled to pay your rent or mortgage for several months. You need to have enough set aside so you and your family can eat. You need to have enough to keep the kids in school and gas in the car.

In Chapter 5 we discuss tools you are going to need to get started. Those alone could add up to more than $1,000. That money comes out of your what-you-need-for-business budget and that is in addition to your we-need-this-to-live-on budget.

Certainly, if you have a spouse who has a steady job, that income will become more important as you start up your new business. Or you might consider initially experiencing the home inspection business on a part-time basis if you can work it around your current job or another steady source of income.

Unfortunately, we can't give you a figure on how much you should have in the bank before you get started. Some people we talked to say you should have at least six months of living expenses set aside before you begin a new venture; others say a one-year cushion is absolutely mandatory. But here's what everybody agreed upon: Many potentially good home inspectors are derailed within the first few months simply because they don't have money in reserve to survive the start-up. More about that in Chapter 22.

You also have the option of going it alone like most inspectors do, going into business with other inspectors (not nearly as common), or buying a "business in a box" as part of a franchise.

Estimates vary on how many inspectors choose the latter route, ranging from 4 percent at a minimum to 10 percent to 15 percent at the high end. Some people consider the franchise option the easiest because it offers ready-made professional literature, contracts, marketing and other documents, along with an instant network of colleagues and a constant source of advice and information.

Of course, the franchise name and support come with a price, such as a percentage of the gross profits. There also may be other disadvantages, like the perception that an independent owner or local owner will provide a better inspection. However, a franchise owner can certainly argue that he or she is locally owned and operated. A franchise also may require that you maintain certain standards that are costlier or more time-consuming than those of your local competitors.

In the end, as in most things, your decision will hinge upon your comfort and confidence levels.

Now the Beginning

For a moment, put aside your visions of working for yourself (true), building a business without being tied to a desk (sort of true), and the freedom to set your own schedule (not always true if you want to make any money).

The most important thing right now is to understand just what a home inspection is supposed to be.

But first, what it's not. It's not an appraisal to determine how much a property is worth. It's not an engineering report of the structural integrity of a home. And it's not the same type of examination that municipal inspectors conduct to determine whether a house or its systems meet local codes or standards.

At its simplest, a home inspection is an objective visual examination of a house, looking at its physical structure and its primary systems, from the foundation all the way up to the roof. That means, in most basic terms, looking at the roof, attic, visible insulation, walls, ceilings, floors, windows, doors, foundation, basement, interior plumbing and electrical systems, the heating system (and possibly the central air-conditioning system), fireplace and chimneys, and grading and drainage. (It's actually more complicated than that, but this gives you a general idea.)

Your task is to use your judgment and experience to give an opinion on whether the components and systems are working as they are intended to and to report any defects that could negatively affect the value of the property or pose a danger to someone—along with your recommendations for monitoring, correcting, or calling in an expert for further evaluation.

You are not required to inspect areas that are not readily accessible. Nor are you expected to put your life in danger or make a prediction on how long the systems and components will continue to function.

Remember: It's not your job to say a house "passes" or "fails" inspection. Your job is to report what you find—the good and the bad—and let someone else (your client) decide what to do next.

Sounds fairly straightforward, right?

Like most things in life, it's not as easy as it seems. There are complicating factors.

First, you don't get to make an inspection in a vacuum. There are other people involved, watching you and waiting for your report, and most definitely evaluating your performance. Your client is usually the prospective buyer or buyers of a house. They may expect you to have X-ray vision, to be all-knowing, and to guarantee the future. It will be your first task to explain the limits of the standard home inspection.

Second, most inspections are an integral part of a real estate transaction. The results could make or break a deal, or cause it to be renegotiated. That means there's probably a great deal of money involved and, undoubtedly, a real estate agent or two who are extremely anxious to make sure you don't kill their chances of making a sale.

There's no question that things can get strange when people and money are involved. We'll delve into that in more detail in later chapters.

For right now, be aware that at the point of the real estate transaction where you come in, the deal is moving at great speed. You likely will be asked to do an inspection within a day or two, preferably yesterday, and chances are good that you will lose the job if you can't fit into someone else's schedule.

Add to that the fact that you probably haven't met your client before you arrive at the house. Even if you do a wonderful job and leave the client happy, the statistics also show that most people live in a house for about eight years. That means you shouldn't expect repeat business from a buyer client for a while. (Although the seller may need an inspection of where he's going—see Chapter 6.)

Also complicating things is the very real possibility that regulatory forces may dictate how you do your work: what you must include in your visual examination and what you aren't required to do.

Currently, there is no federal oversight of the home inspection industry. But states have begun to regulate inspectors operating within their borders. The regulations may be as restrictive as demanding that you have a high school diploma or equivalency, that you purchase a certain level of liability or errors and omissions insurance, and that your inspection includes specific things. A state also might say that anyone with an engineering degree is exempt from any home inspection requirements. Or the regulations may be as loose as allowing anyone to obtain an inspector's license for little more than paying the fee. And of course, there are some states that lack any kind of regulation or laws even mentioning home inspectors.

You'll need to check with your state to find out what it expects from you, if anything. Most states have a licensing board or agency you can contact, or you could ask one of the national home inspector organizations because they generally monitor state licensing activities. (See Chapter 17 for information on these groups.)

Like many states, the organizations also may have some ideas on how you should perform a home inspection. Most have "standards of practice" spelling out what they think you should include and what you don't have to, and will urge you to relay those standards to your clients. These groups ask you to voluntarily agree to these principles in exchange for the privilege of calling yourself a member and using the group's logo to enhance your credibility.

Another complicating factor is the threat of being sued by an unhappy buyer who wants to blame someone for problems with a new home. Following state requirements and/or an organization's "standards of practice" are important, as is doing an extremely thorough job. Expertise, whether from experience or through training, is crucial.

Now, to what you really want to know.

The answer is most definitely "no."

You don't have to come out of the construction industry to be a good home inspector.

In fact, there are some people who think a construction background can be a detriment. Others believe becoming a home inspector will be easier if you have an interest in the home industry, even if it's no more than the fact that you enjoy puttering around your own house or making trips to the local home improvement store. And as you might expect, there also are those who are adamant that you should have some background in at least one of the areas that you will be inspecting—plumbing, electricity, roofing, and so on.

The reality is that home inspectors today come from all walks of life. Why not yours?

But forget about background and expertise for a moment.

Skills can be learned. Personality cannot.

What the experts agree upon is this: If you don't like people and you don't communicate well with others, this most definitely is not the profession for you.

"Doing a home inspection is a science, but explaining it is an art," says Janice Ruhs, who with her husband owns the World Inspection Network of Green Hills/Brentwood in Hermitage, Tennessee.

It goes without saying that home inspection requires an eye for detail. Communication skills become vital when you find a problem.

"You have to be detail-oriented and able to communicate very well with people who don't understand the magnitude of the findings," says Michael Casey, an 18-year home inspector from Haymarket, Virginia.

"You have to be able to communicate negative information in a positive fashion. I do not advocate a home inspector going light—going unethical. The method of delivery is important. You have to use the Joe Friday approach—state the facts—and not be emotional.

"If a house needs a lot of work, the customer should understand the magnitude. You can tell them there are different options for correction of the problems. The customer needs to understand that."

Casey is among those who believe a contracting or construction background isn't always a plus for new home inspectors.

"I run an inspection training school and we have 11 schools across the country. We find that people who don't have preexisting opinions simply are better at being home inspectors," he says. "You can be taught to be a home inspector."

Jay Schnoor of Professional Home Inspection Company Inc. in La Crescent, Minnesota, agrees. "One of the best inspectors I've employed had zero background in construction. He was inquisitive, willing to learn, and had a very good rapport with people. I think it's 50-50. Technical knowledge can be learned. Skills with people are difficult to learn. They have to be genetic, almost."

Lynette Gebben of Madison, Wisconsin, also believes in the same ratio.

"I wish I could say it was 80 percent technical, but only 20 percent consumer service. But it's really more like 50-50. You have to have a good knowledge with the technical area and a very good rapport with speaking with the public."

Gebben also says a home inspector must be able to climb a ladder, crawl in a crawlspace, and not mind the diversity of home types, their age, or adverse conditions.

(A few words here about "adverse conditions" beyond the expected stages of disrepair or mud and filth. Being a home inspector also can require personal courage. It isn't always easy climbing a ladder to inspect a very high roof, or inching your way into a narrow, dark crawlspace that may also be home to creatures like spiders and mice. Or exploring attics inhabited by bats and basements that have attracted rats or snakes. Sometimes you may have to contend with creatures of nature that fly—and sting—like bees and wasps. You can read more about death-defying home inspections in Chapter 12.)

On the other side, John Merritt, a former contractor who now owns an AmeriSpec franchise in Santa Rosa, California, believes his background as a remodeling contractor has been invaluable.

"You need to have a knowledge of how houses are built and you need to know the kinds of problems that do occur in houses," says Merritt. But he agrees that temperament is important, along with an ability to deal with stress. "There are some very stressful situations. In doing a home inspection, you are dealing with buyers and sellers who are under a lot of stress."

Merritt says there is no doubt that you will need training—and in different areas.

"You need to do some pretty intensive training on how to inspect things. You need training on legal issues, how the real estate transaction uses inspectors, some computer training, and if you are a single operator, you need some business and accounting training, Internet training because everyone uses the Internet and e-mail, and you will need some sales training on how to sell your services."

Stan Garnet of Inspectors Associates Inc., in Atlanta, Georgia, who also is involved in home inspection training, agrees that learning to be a home inspector these days goes beyond the ability to examine a house.

"If you intend to be successful in this business, you need marketing skills, you need communication skills, and you need computer skills. If you don't have those, you better hire the people that do have them."

CHAPTER 3

What Do You Need to Know?

And where can you go to learn it?

Assan inspector, the breadth and depth of your inspections will vary, depending on what state you're in, what organization's standards of practice you follow, and what your company wants included in the inspection (if you're not the owner).

In addition, you may decide your inspections will go beyond the "standards of practice." Or you may be asked by a client to add things, and then you will have to decide whether you'll agree to it for free—or a fee.

In most general terms, no matter what, as an inspector you will use various methods to examine these systems of a house:

- Exterior
- Structural
- Roofing
- Electrical
- Heating and cooling
- Insulating and ventilation
- Plumbing
- Interior
- Fireplace and chimney

When inspecting a house you will rely on your senses, specifically on sight, smell, touch, and hearing. You will also need to be at ease with taking things apart and with using probes and other special instruments and/or processes to determine the condition of not-readily accessible systems and components.

Those states and organizations that want to ensure a home inspection meets certain criteria will spell out the things you must include. They also may require that you first obtain a specific number of hours of training. (The American Society of Home Inspectors [ASHI] model legislation that it wants states to adopt calls for 80 hours of instruction, at least 25 supervised inspections, and continuing education.) Some states also require that you have a high school education or a GED before you even begin studying to be a home inspector.

And when you're finished with your training, the states and organizations may want you to pass a technical examination before you begin inspecting houses.

The National Home Inspector Examination (NHIE), administered by an independent board since 1999, is one test accepted by a number of states and organizations and provides a good insight into what you, as an inspector, should know before you hang out your shingle and get your business cards printed up.

To give you a basic idea, the test covers four areas you will be required to be knowledgeable about:

1. Inspection Methods
2. Building Systems (including exterior, structural, roofing, electrical, heating and cooling, insulating and ventilating, plumbing, interior, and fireplace and chimney systems)
3. Reporting
4. Professional Practice

Generally speaking, you will be expected to know the common types of each of the building systems it tests your knowledge on, as well as the typical defects. You also will be expected to be aware of maintenance concerns and procedures, as well as safety issues, applicable standards, and appropriate terminology.

By taking a look at this test, you will get a better idea of the wide range of inspection areas that will face you on the job. Along with the categories you would expect—such as roofs, wiring, and foundations—you also have to know about things like driveways, drainage, how air moves in a house, and countertops, for example.

Simply put: Being a house inspector requires a great deal of knowledge about a great many things that make up a house.

For more detailed information on the NHIE, visit the NHIE Web site at *www.homeinspectionexam.org.* The Web site also includes suggested reading and a sample test.

If you decide to pursue this test to get your license, NHIE has more than 180 test centers across the country where you will have up to four hours to complete the 200-question multiple-choice test on a personal computer. The cost is around $195, and veterans are reimbursed by the Department of Veterans Affairs.

How Do You Learn This Stuff?

Feeling overwhelmed yet? Don't be.

As Michael Casey, a former ASHI president who hails from Virginia, notes, "Houses are built pretty much the same, just with different materials."

Stephen Gladstone of Stamford, Connecticut, offers another perspective:

"In my mind, the best way to approach this business is that it's simple, but not simplistic. You need to be able to give the consumer an important mix of information about the property that is going to be crucial in that consumer's life. It's extraordinarily important that people learn their craft."

Even before getting into the specialties of electrical work, plumbing, roofing systems and the rest, Gladstone says inspectors need to have good deductive reasoning skills. "You have to understand how a home is constructed—not how it is built—so that you understand how systems fit together. A stain on the ceiling might come from a leak in an upstairs pipe, but the pipe might be leaking because the foundation has shifted. You need to be able to put all those things together.

> "**Y**ou are constantly going to be learning about new types of equipment. You're going to be sitting on the Internet, looking at new products and going down to Home Depot to see how much things cost," says Gladstone. ■

"Over the last 20 years, it has become assumed by the client that the inspector will look at the whole gamut of things and be expert in each one," he says.

New people entering the business need to be able to do research.

The consumer expects you to know these things.

Now that you have a general idea of what you are expected to learn, how do you go about learning it?

There is a myriad of ways to get trained in this business, not the least of which are formal classes and schools to train home inspectors. You should locate reputable sources of training through state licensing agencies, which have approved lists of training courses, or through home inspector organizations.

The costs vary, but expect to pay at least $1,000 and probably closer to $3,000.

The training time also will vary; some programs want you to devote several days straight, others will stretch out the training time over several weeks. Some programs require that you obtain all of your education at their training sites, some offer distance education where you train via computers and the Internet, some are workbook-based, and many others use various combinations of these methods. In other words, you have options and the opportunity to choose a training program that will fit best into your current circumstances.

If you decide to buy an inspection franchise, you'll likely be offered training from the parent company, and again, the time required and the method of delivery will vary from franchise to franchise.

You may have seen ads for correspondence courses, often linked to promises of easy wealth. Tread cautiously here. Some states are specific about the kind of training you should have and where it comes from. To find top-quality approved schools, you can always go to Dearborn's home inspection Web site, *www.dearbornhomeinspection.com*. (There are other excellent distance learning opportunities, but make sure they meet your state's standards.)

Remember: You want to be sure that your training prepares you to pass the technical exam required by your state so that you can (1) get your license and (2) include your training in your marketing campaign.

Another way to prepare for plunging into the home inspection business is to be an apprentice to another inspector; some states even require it. This allows you to "learn by doing" and by observing an expert in the field and watching how he or she deals with the unexpected. Remember: Although all houses are basically built in the same way, *no two houses are exactly alike*. That also means no two house inspections are going to be exactly the same, either.

But that is what can make this profession so challenging and so interesting.

Following are some of the topics listed on the NHIE. This list should provide you with a good idea of the topics that home inspectors should know about. In each of the topics, you will be expected to know about the following:

- Common types
- Materials
- Applications
- Installation methods
- Construction techniques
- Typical defects
- Maintenance concerns
- Procedures
- Safety issues
- Applicable standards
- Appropriate terminology

Here are the categories covered in the NHIE and some of the additional factors you will need to be aware of during an inspection.

Exterior Systems

Vegetation, grading, drainage, and retaining walls, including

- typical vegetation and landscape conditions, and mainte-nance practices and how they may affect the building

Driveways, patios, and walkways

Decks, balconies, stoops, stairs, steps, porches, and applicable railings

Wall cladding, flashing, trim, eaves, soffits, and fascia, including

- common types (e.g., plywood, aluminum cladding, step flashing, composite siding, SIPS [Structural Insulated Panel Systems], EIFS [Exterior Insulation and Finish Systems])
- typical defects (e.g., nailing, water absorption)
- appropriate inspection tools and their uses (e.g., probe, awl, moisture meter)

Exterior doors and windows

Structural Systems

Foundation, including

- common foundation types, materials, applications, installation methods, and construction techniques
- typical foundation system modifications, repairs, upgrades, and retrofit methods and materials
- common foundation conditions and defects (e.g., cracks, settlement) and their common causes and effects
- soil types and conditions and how they affect foundation types
- applied forces and how they affect foundation systems (e.g., wind, seismic, loads)
- safety issues, applicable standards, and appropriate terminology

Floor structure, including

- common floor system types (e.g., trusses, concrete slabs, joists), materials, applications, installation methods, and construction techniques
- typical modifications, repairs, upgrades, and retrofits methods and materials
- typical defects (e.g., improper cuts and notches in structural members)
- limitations of framing materials (e.g., span)
- applied forces and how they affect floor systems (e.g., wind, seismic, loads)

Walls and vertical support structures, including

- seismic and wind-resistant construction methods and hardware
- fire blocking

Ceilings, including

- acceptable truss and ceiling structural-member modifications, repairs, upgrades, and retrofits methods, and materials
- limitations of framing materials (e.g., span)
- applied forces and how they affect ceiling structures (e.g., wind, seismic, loads)

Roofing Systems

Roofs, including

- limitations of framing materials (e.g., span)
- seismic and wind-resistant construction and hardware
- insufficient ventilation and how it affects roof structures
- applied forces and how they affect roof structures (e.g., wind, seismic, loads)
- cathedral ceilings and how they affect roof framing

Roof covering, including

- deck and sheathing requirements for different types of roof coverings

Roof drainage systems, including

- typical defects such as ponding, improper slopes, and disposal of water runoff

Flashings

Skylights and other roof penetrations, including

- common skylight and other roof penetration types, materials, applications, installation methods, and construction techniques

Electrical Systems

Service drop of service lateral, service equipment, and service grounding, including

- typical defects (e.g., water and rust in panel equipment, height)
- electrical service capacity
- service grounding and bonding

Interior components of service panels and subpanels, including

- main disconnects
- panel grounding and subpanel neutral isolation
- panel wiring
- over-current protection devices
- function of circuit breakers and fuses
- inspection safety procedures

Wiring systems, including

- problems with aluminum wire
- obsolete electrical wiring system

Devices, equipment, and fixtures (e.g., switches, receptacles, lights), including

- equipment grounding
- wiring, operation, location of typical devices and equipment (e.g., air conditioners, arc fault; GFCI [Ground-Fault Circuit Interrupters])

Heating and Cooling Systems

Heating and cooling, including

- theory of refrigerant cycle (latent and sensible heat)
- theory of heat transfer and how it takes place in different heating system types
- theory of equipment sizing
- methods of testing the systems
- performance parameters
- condensate control and disposal
- by-products of combustion, their generation, and how and when they become a safety hazard

Distribution systems

Venting systems, including

- theory of venting
- equipment sizing

Insulating and Ventilating Systems

Thermal insulation, including

- theory of heat transfer and energy conservation
- performance parameters (e.g., R-value)

Moisture management, including

- evidence or conditions for mold
- theory of moisture generation and movement
- performance parameters
- vapor pressure and its effects
- theory of relative humidity

- effects of moisture on building components, occupants, and indoor air quality
- moisture control systems
- appearance or indications of excessive moisture
- likely locations for condensation to occur

Ventilation systems of attics, crawlspaces, roof assemblies, and interior spaces, including

- typical ventilation defects and how they affect buildings and people
- theory of air movement
- theory of relative humidity
- air movement in building assemblies
- interdependence of mechanical systems and ventilation systems
- appliance vent systems requirements (e.g., dryers, range hoods)
- screening, sizing, and location requirements for vent openings

Plumbing Systems

Water supply distribution system, including

- common water pressure/flow problems and how they affect the water distribution system
- pipe deterioration issues (e.g., PVC, galvanized, brass)

Fixtures and faucets

Drain, waste, and vent systems, including

- theory and usage of traps and vents
- acceptable piping, materials, and applications
- indications of defective venting or drain slope
- identification of public or private disposal (when possible)
- joining dissimilar pipe materials
- proper support spacing

Water heating systems, including

- typical water heater defects (e.g., improper vent/flue materials, condition, unsafe locations, connections)
- accessory items (e.g., drain pans, seismic restraints)
- connections to and controls for energy source
- combustion air requirements
- vent exhaust air spillage

Fuel storage and fuel distribution systems, including

- defects in above-ground oil/gas storage tanks
- fuel leak indications, repairs, and remediation methods
- basic components of gas appliance valves and their functions
- tank restraints and supports
- underground storage tank indicators and reporting requirements

Drainage sumps, sump pumps, sewage ejection pumps, and related piping, including

- sump pump location significance
- pump discharge location significance
- wiring installation methods

Interior Systems

Walls, ceiling, floors, doors, and windows, including

- types of defects in interior surfaces not caused by defects in other systems
- typical defects in interior surfaces caused by defects in other systems

Walls, ceiling, floors, doors, windows, and related fire/life safety equipment, including

- egress requirements
- applicable fire/safety and occupancy separation requirements (e.g., smoke detectors, window bars, ladders, firewalls, fire doors, and penetrations)

- operation of windows, doors, window bars, and other fire/life safety equipment and components

Steps, stairways, landings and railings

Installed countertops and cabinets, including

- common cabinet and countertop types, materials, applications, installation methods, and construction techniques

Garage doors and operators

Fireplace and Chimney Systems

Fireplaces, solid-fuel burning appliances, chimneys, and vents, including

- common manufactured fireplaces and solid-fuel-burning appliance types, materials, applications, installation methods, and construction techniques
- common manufactured fireplaces and solid-fuel-burning appliance chimney, vent connector, and vent types, materials, applications, installation methods, and construction techniques of direct-vent and non-vented fireplaces
- common masonry fireplace types, materials, applications, installation methods, and construction techniques
- common direct-vent fireplace vent types, materials, applications, installation methods, and construction techniques
- chimney terminations (e.g., spark arrestors)
- chimney height and clearance requirements
- theory of heat transfer and fire safety fundamentals
- effects of moisture and excessive heat on fireplaces
- fuel types and combustion characteristics
- combustion air supply requirements
- operation of equipment, components, and accessories

CHAPTER 4

Home Inspection: It Isn't Just a Man's World

There's no reason why women can't succeed,
and thrive, in this business.

By now, you already know that if you're afraid of the dark, spider webs, or climbing ladders, you might as well put down this book and walk away. You also should know by now that you don't need muscles built up from working in construction or another related trade to succeed in this business.

These things are true, whether you are a man or a woman.

Even though home inspection can be a path to fame and fortune for anyone, not many women choose to enter this industry. But there is no reason why they shouldn't.

"My personal feeling is that women perceive it as a dirty sort of job. Perhaps there is a misunderstanding of what the day-in and day-out is all about," says Michelle Teague of All About Homes LLC, who used her Master of Business Administration skills to launch a thriving home inspection business in Chicago. "I think that some women aren't interested in getting dirty, or they don't know about homes.

"But I've had a lots of jobs. And this is the greatest job I've ever had."

It goes without saying that historically, the home inspection business has been dominated by men. But there's no reason you can't be one of the women who are slowly but surely entering the profession and quickly finding success.

You'll probably discover what they've discovered: Many times, being female gives you a distinct advantage. Every once in a while it can be a hindrance. But *most of the time*, it makes no difference at all.

Sure, you may encounter a good ol' boy or two who doesn't believe a woman can do the job. But odds are good that you'll find their doubts quickly fading once they see you're a skilled home inspector *first,* and a woman *second.* (Within the industry, women report few problems from male colleagues, but some say it took licensing restrictions to weed out less-than-professional male chauvinists.)

Mardi Clissold of Home Critic in Austin, Texas says in only a "handful of times" out of more than 1,500 inspections has her gender been an issue with clients.

"It's usually been older men, and then they see that I know what I'm talking about," she says.

Her advice to women considering the profession is to be aware that "sometimes you will be tested."

"It's real important to be confident and to show you know what you're doing," says Clissold. "You really need to be professional."

That's also been the experience of Janice Ruhs, who joined her husband in 1997 in opening a franchise in Hermitage, Tennessee. She became Tennessee's first female home inspector and then the first woman nationwide to earn the National Association of Home Inspectors' Certified Real Estate Inspector designation.

"I did have a young gal buying a home and her dad was there. From the expression on his face, you could tell he was not happy. That's OK. I start the inspection process and after about 15 or 20 minutes, he sees that I'm there to do the job.

"The language and knowledge that I bring to the table is what they're looking for."

Diane Marotz, a registered nurse turned home inspector in Madison, Wisconsin, agrees. She quotes one gentleman who said, "When I found Diane in the phone book, I figured any woman who was going to get into a predominantly male-dominated career had to know what they were doing to stay up with that group."

"The public, I think, is pretty good with it," Marotz says. "People are sort of surprised at what got you into this. They say things like, 'Gee, I wouldn't want to crawl around in the cobwebs,' and all those kinds of stereotypical things. But this job is easier on my body physically than nursing was."

Like their male counterparts, women home inspectors come from all walks of life. Many believe a background in home construction is not required, but some familiarity with a facet or two of the homebuilding industry—either directly or through a loved one—is a plus (just as it is for men). Also, possibly like you, some women are simply drawn to the idea of building their own business without being chained to a desk. They enjoy encountering new situations every day and want the freedom of setting their own schedules (which can be an advantage if children are part of their lives).

Quite often, female inspectors say that the "female eye for detail" and "an innate intuitiveness" may make it easier for women to do a thorough inspection and then communicate the results, both negative and positive, in a way that clients can understand and appreciate.

And it doesn't hurt to go beyond what's expected and offer a few little extra bits of knowledge. Alyssa Hickson of National Home Inspection Corp. in Malabar, Florida, says she often advises clients on ways they can save money, such as reducing home insurance rates by something as simple as making sure they have the right kind of hoses on the washing machine or smoke detectors in every room.

"Sometimes it's important for women to have an edge," she says, "knowing a little bit more and knowing as much as any contractor."

And like the men out there, you need to remember that another major factor in your success will be the relationships you build with local real estate agents (more on this in Chapter 7).

Fortunately for you, the National Association of REALTORS® says the majority of those real estate agents (55 percent) are women. And that can be a real advantage, especially when you're just starting out.

Kimberly St. Louis, a financial analyst who opened an A-Pro Home Inspection Services franchise office in Madison, Wisconsin, in 2001, agrees. "When I first started, on my list of pros and cons I had being female on the con side. Now it's definitely on the pro side." ■

"Women real estate agents have given me a chance where they wouldn't have if I had not been a woman," says Teague of her Chicago-area business.

Hickson confirms that the female factor can be important.

"A lot of real estate agents are female. And they feel more comfortable having a woman there. Most of the time, the client isn't even there, it's the real estate agent," she says.

As a female home inspector, you also can profit from a growing trend: More women are buying houses, and often these women know a woman can do an inspection as well as a man.

There also are a lot of men who prefer to deal with a female home inspector.

"I find a lot more men are more comfortable with a woman doing inspections," says Marotz, of Home Inspecting Partner Inc. "A lot more people are not as familiar with the trades as they used to be. A number of men don't really know anything about a roof, furnace, or whatever. They feel comfortable asking a woman. Sometimes they feel, 'As a guy I should know this.' Maybe a guy doesn't want to ask another guy what's going on.

"I think in general a lot of people are much more comfortable talking to a woman," she says. "Even for sellers it may be more comfortable knowing a woman is coming into their home. Other women feel more comfortable with women as well. People who have children are comfortable with a woman doing an inspection."

"It's such a male-dominated industry. I feel that a lot of women feel like they are getting ripped off a lot. And who books the home inspections? The female. The husband says, 'Take care of it.' Also, in Madison, so many female businesswomen own their own homes."

Safety First

She, like Teague, works alone and sometimes has concerns about her physical safety when working alone in very rural areas. Teague admits to concerns in some urban areas as well.

"I've never felt in danger because of the inspection itself, but I have been in neighborhoods where I felt unsafe. But I think men would have felt unsafe too," she said. "In any city there are pockets that are not good places to be by yourself."

The problem for any inspector (male or female) is what to do when you find yourself in such a position—and there are no easy answers.

No matter how well you think you know a city, you may not know a specific area is a tough part of town when the phone rings and a client wants to set up an appointment. Even worse, you may find it very hard to back out of an appointment once you've discovered the concern: Remember, the client is likely to be on a tight deadline to get the inspection completed before the contract expires. The buyer and the sales agent are likely to have arranged their schedules so they can participate in the inspection at a specific time on a specific day.

If you drive into a neighborhood you don't like, it's not going to be as easy as just driving back out.

"I like to arrive at the house before the appointed time," Teague says. "That way I can get started on the outside inspection before anyone else gets there. But that means I'm there by myself—a young blonde girl with thousands of dollars worth of equipment in the car. You have guys from the street come up to you and try to back you into a corner. There have been times when I wished I brought a can of Mace with me."

Although some women home inspectors put their pictures in the phone book or on their advertising materials, others do not because of safety concerns. Many take precautions, like making sure a real estate agent also is on the property during the inspection or that the owner is there if it is a For Sale By Owner situation.

Other female home inspectors join husbands or other male relatives in the business. For Shelly Barroner, a former full-time homemaker now working with her husband in Williamsburg, Pennsylvania, that also means doing joint inspections.

"My husband does the attic and basement areas and outside. He takes care of the major areas that he does have expertise in, like heating and plumbing. I do the inside of the house, check for leaks, check the windows and doors, look at all the interior surfaces," she says.

Ruhs says she also started out that way, but now finds it's easier and more profitable if both do inspections solo. But she concedes that a smaller physique can be a bit of a disadvantage when working alone.

"There's nothing I can't do but it sometimes takes me longer. I'm 5′1″ and 100 pounds. Most guys can just lift the ladder off the top of their vehicle but I have to get a ladder to get the ladder."

The only other disadvantage?

"I can never find designer crawlspace coveralls that fit."

CHAPTER 5

Tools of the Trade

Let's talk start-up costs.

O
K, you think to yourself, how much money do I really
need to invest to do this job? After all, you once
watched your brother-in-law repair an electrical socket, so you're
pretty sure that with just a little extra training you could be a
home inspector. (How tough can it be?)

Even better, around the house somewhere you think you've
probably got all the tools you need. It's just a matter of gathering
them up, throwing them into a bag, and heading off to a property.
(All right, maybe just a quick stop at the hardware store to pick up
a few extra things.) But otherwise, you're definitely good to go.

Right?

Well, as your old high school coach might have said, "If it was
that easy, we'd get someone else to do it."

For the modern home inspector, the tools of the trade go way
beyond a ladder, a flashlight, and a couple of screwdrivers. (But
make no mistake: you do need a ladder, a flashlight, and a couple
of screwdrivers, for starters.) In fact, before you ever step into
someone's home, you could have anywhere from several hundred
to several thousand dollars invested in the tools of your trade,

which can be a pretty hefty sum considering that you've yet to collect a single fee.

As you go through your career, your inventory of tools is going to multiply. And if you end up specializing in a tangent discipline—environmental testing, lead-based paint testing, and so on—you could quickly see the variety and value of your "basic tools" soar into the tens of thousands of dollars.

So before you get any business cards printed up, it might be a good idea to take this list down to the local home improvement center to get a glimpse of what you're getting yourself into.

Getting Started

Over the years we've talked to a number of home inspectors about the tools they use. Invariably, Rule 1 is always "Don't go cheap." You don't have to get the top of the line, at least to start with, but cheap tools that break (or worse, cause damage to a property) do far more harm that good, and if we're talking about measuring devices for things like water pressure or electrical current, they can be inaccurate.

As is true with almost anything these days, and certainly for almost everything on the list below, prices can easily run from a comparative handful of dollars to several hundred, depending on the manufacturer, the quality, and how many things you want it to do. Electrical circuit testers can run from very cheap to very expensive. Gas sniffers also come in a wide range of prices.

So if you're just starting out, think "quality," think "middle price range," think "maybe there's a sale coming up." And don't forget, there are deals all over the Internet. Check them out.

Here is a short list of things you could find yourself in need of as you move into your career:

- *Binoculars:* Small (11-power) binoculars. You're going to need these to look at roofs that you either can't, or won't, walk on. $30 or more.
- *Digital camera:* More and more, inspectors will take pictures of problems they see so that they can explain them more

easily to their clients. Plus, said one inspector, "Sometimes I take pictures when I run into something and say, 'Jeez, what is that thing?' I can study it back in the office, or send it to another inspector for a second opinion." Nothing under 3 megapixels. $200 to $300 (and coming down).

- *Electrical circuit analyzer, arc fault, ground fault circuit testers, sensor pens:* You'll be plugging devices into wall outlets to check the current and for other problems. Sensor pens also are popular items. They glow as you approach a live wire. Electrical equipment: prices are in a wide range. Plan to spend a few hundred dollars.

- *Flashlights:* A couple of flashlights. Like ladders, a lot of inspectors like to carry both large and small versions. A large, 25,000-candlepower flashlight can throw a lot of light into an attic, crawlspace, or other unlighted area. You might want to consider one that is lightweight and rechargeable. Probably around $100. There are going to be times, however, when you're going to need less candlepower—when you're looking under sinks, for instance—so you're going to want something smaller. Again, think reliability and probably rechargeability. You should be able to find what you need in the $20 range.

- *Gas leak detector and carbon monoxide tester:* $180 to $300.

- *Inspection mirror:* An inspection mirror is a lot like a dental mirror (but much larger) and serves a similar purpose—to see what's on the other side of something that you can't get your head around to see directly. Figure $20.

- *Ladder:* One, maybe two, ladders. Most inspectors say they need a good quality extension ladder that can reach up to at least 22 feet. This is high enough to reach most roofs, and even climb up on a roof if you absolutely have to. Many inspectors also carry 6-foot stepladders for use inside the house to get a better look at ceiling lights, ceiling fans, and to inspect water spots and cracks. Do not be chintzy when buying a ladder. It's not unusual for inspectors to spend $450 to $500 on a large ladder (many prefer the "Little Giant" brand). Be sure to keep a couple of things in mind: The ladder needs to be heavy enough so that when you put it up against a building, it will stay there; a slight breeze won't blow it down, which would leave you, well, up. But it also needs to be light enough so that you can move it with some ease, to say nothing of loading and unloading it from your vehicle several times a day. Also good to keep in mind is that fiberglass ladders tend to cause fewer scratches than metal ones, and the seller is going to appreciate that.

- *Level:* You'll probably want both a short level (six inches or so) and a long one (up to a couple of feet). You'll be checking whether floors and stairs are level, and the slope of pipes. (For demonstration purposes, some inspectors also are known to carry a marble that they can set in the middle of a floor and let it roll to show a buyer just how far off level the floor may be.) Usually not too expensive for small levels.

- *Mallet:* A plastic mallet. You're going to find yourself tapping on floors and ceramic tiles around bathtubs, showers, and in the kitchen, looking for anything that may be loose. You don't need anything too exotic here, as long as it doesn't leave a mark on what you're tapping. Should be less than $10.

- *Moisture meter:* These are used to measure dampness where there shouldn't be any—water coming in through ceilings, seeping into basements, and so on. Around $150.

- *Paintbrush:* A small paintbrush. This will probably be one of the cheapest tools in your arsenal and one that you actually may have around the house. You're not going to be painting anything, of course. You'll use the small paintbrush to brush away dust, dirt, paint chips, spider webs, and that sort of thing so that you can get a better look at wiring connections, pipes, inside furnaces, and so on.

- *Pocket knife:* Many inspectors carry something of the Swiss Army variety with a variety of tools built in. $30.

- *Screwdrivers:* Flathead and Phillips screwdrivers. Some inspectors like the so-called six-way screwdrivers that include various head styles for various jobs. Also pretty popular are multiheaded power screwdrivers that can be real time and energy savers when you're unscrewing something like the front panel on an electrical box (64 treads per inch).

Again, rechargeable screwdrivers come in a wide price range. Something in the area of $30 should do you.

- *Shoes:* Good solid work shoes. Wearing sneakers on a roof with any degree of slope is an invitation to disaster. Sneakers are the worst possible shoes to wear on any roof. Sturdy shoes (with an arch support) will save your life. Around $100 to $120. But don't forget that after you are done walking around outside, you still have to walk around inside. If you don't want to track dirt inside the house, which home sellers really don't want you to do, you will either want to put on a different pair of shoes to inspect the interior or slip on some shoe coverings. About $20.

- *Tape measure:* You're going to need a good quality tape measure, metal, rigid, probably in the 12-foot to 25-foot range, to measure everything from furnace clearance to inches of attic insulation. Your clients are going to want to borrow it to make room and window measurements while they're there. An electronic measurer is a kind of neat "gee whiz" tool that can impress your clients. Tape measures usually aren't very expensive

- *Thermometer:* Thermometer to read water temperatures. $180.

- *Toolbox:* You're going to need some easy way to carry your tools. A toolbox or carrying case of some kind will cost $20 or $30—more if you want it personalized with your name or company logo.

- *Vehicle:* Something to carry everything else in. A company-owned vehicle dedicated almost exclusively to business is virtually a necessity nowadays. At any given time, you need to carry thousands of dollars worth of equipment to your jobs. Pickup trucks are the cliché, and are viewed with less favor than large SUVs. SUVs are enclosed and protected from weather and itinerants. But either one is better than trying to pile all your stuff into your Mustang convertible. Also, any vehicle may get you to the job site, but not all vehicles carry the same hint of prestige. Real estate agents have preferences for BMWs and Mercedes because they silently speak to the quality of the agent. Many home inspectors drive new, large SUVs for the same reason. Some inspectors are even known to drive Hummers because they feel that vehicle makes a certain statement about their status in the industry. And don't forget, signs and lettering on the sides of vehicles could be an important marketing tool—and all of these things come at a price.

- *Water pressure meter:* For checking the water pressure in the house. About $30.
- *Work clothes:* More on this a few more paragraphs down, but for basics you may want some coveralls, safety gloves, inexpensive rubber dishwashing-type gloves, safety glasses. Not too expensive.
- *And assorted unseens:* Does your state require you to carry errors and omissions insurance, which as a higher-risk, first-year inspector, could cost you more than $3,500 per year? Does your state require you to have a license? Do you need to be bonded? Also, are you going to insure your tools and your business? Are you going to cover yourself with medical insurance?

And Then There's That Pesky Professionalism

You can see that the basics you need to inspect a home can add up fairly quickly. But beyond that, there are expenses necessary to run almost any business, and even other expenses beyond those that are best placed under the category of "professionalism."

For instance, you are going to need a modern computer with access to the Internet. Two of the tools of your business are going to be your Web site (where you will post those glowing references from previous clients) and your ability to send and receive e-mail (and do try to respond to your e-mail promptly). Add on top of that a good quality printer for producing reports for your clients. Don't forget the cost of the software that will include templates that will help produce those reports.

Many modern home inspection services also are using computer tablets these days—small, handheld computers with "checklist" software installed so that you can "check off" issues on the computer form as you move through a house. Those tablets may connect to a portable printer ($250), so that the entire report can be prepared, printed, and delivered to the client before you leave the premises.

Once you are in business, you are going to want to tell people you are in business. Advertising in the local newspaper can be expensive, depending on the size of the newspaper. You may want to advertise in the Yellow Pages, the cost of which can mount up quickly, or just give flyers to local real estate companies or even consumers. Remember, you're not really in business unless other people know you're in business.

Also, don't forget that you are going to need a cell phone. Good quality cell phones have become an indispensable tool for making appointments, breaking appointments, and working out issues (before they become issues) with clients and real estate agents. (*Question: Do you turn off your cell phone during an inspection, or leave it on? There has been some debate concerning this issue.* More on phones in Chapter 6.)

If you have a cell phone, you may be able to get along without a pager. (People will call you rather than page you.) Some inspectors say they like to have both.

You will likely need a business phone in your office. If you have a home office, as many home inspectors do, you probably will want a separate line dedicated to just business calls. Extra lines cost extra money. If you use your home phone line as your business line, you run the risk of your teenager tying up your phone while your clients are trying to contact you. (Some inspectors try to get away with using their cell phone as their "business line." You might be able to do that, but only if service is very reliable.)

With any luck, you are not usually going to be in your office answering the phone. You'll be out doing jobs. That means either an answering machine or a person to take your messages. (Rule of thumb here is that machines are cheaper labor than humans, but people would rather talk to humans than machines. What does your budget allow?)

Fax machines can be built into computers or can be bought as a stand-alone piece of hardware. You may need a fax machine so you are able to send reports to clients.

Don't forget there are three-in-one devices that fax, photocopy, and print. These three-in-one devices can save you some money.

There also are expenses that you will need to undertake that are as much a part of the business as an electric screwdriver.

If you are serious about your profession, you will want to join at least one of the organizations discussed in Chapter 17. Figure as much as a couple of hundred dollars for some of those memberships.

There is a constant need for education and training and a constant need to keep yourself abreast of what's happening in the industry, so add a couple of thousand dollars per year in travel to professional meetings and conferences.

Back home, if you want to be seen as a professional, you'll want to dress like a professional. That may mean wearing khakis instead of blue jeans on the job. It also may mean shirts monogrammed with your name and company logo. And, of course, not just one shirt and pants combination. Odds are you will be getting dirty at every home you inspect (there is no such thing as a clean crawlspace), and the job can be plenty hot and sweaty. You are likely going to want to put on clean clothes before going to each new job. And if you don't want to wash your clothes every night of your life, you are going to have to lay out some serious money for multiples of shirts and pants. Consider it your business wardrobe.

So how much can you expect to spend just to stay in business? Well, there certainly are ways to economize, and the longer you've been in business, the more efficient you become and the more you are able to amortize the cost of your tools over the number of jobs you have.

Nevertheless, some inspectors believe their overhead comes to $2,500 per month—money spent before a single dollar comes in.

Bottom line (literally): **Start stockpiling cash.**

Market Thyself

You may be a great home inspector, but
nobody will know it unless you sell yourself.

Once you decide to become a home inspector, how are you going to find homes to inspect? Saying you're a home inspector isn't going to be enough to make your phone ring.

Sure, home inspectors are an integral part of the real estate transaction. And yes, about three-fourths of all home sales include inspections these days. And of course, that number is expected to continue to rise. With millions of homes bought and sold every year, this seems like a pretty good business to be part of.

But how are you going to find the homes and how are they going to find you?

You are going to have to market yourself. There is no other way.

That includes the traditional avenues used by most businesses: ads in the phone book and the newspaper, business cards, brochures, and so on, to make sure your name is out there and findable. It also means braving the Internet because so many of today's buyers are doing most of their research on the Web. In addition, you must make the other parties in the real estate transaction, such as real estate agents and mortgage bankers, aware that you exist while at the same time carefully avoiding any behavior that could be viewed as unethical or illegal, such as offering kickbacks.

Where to begin?

If you have decided to buy a home inspection franchise, a great deal of this likely will already be done for you as part of your "business in a box." You will be able to sell your services on the coattails of the franchise name, using the franchise's suggested marketing materials, and that can make things easier. (The downside here, of course, is that you don't get to keep all your profits because the franchise is going to want some of them.)

However, even if you are part of a franchise, you won't be the only home inspector operating out there.

For you to keep your doors open, you need business and you need a business plan. And until you've been in home inspection long enough that you can fill an appointment book with referrals, marketing will be essential to your success. You could hire a marketing specialist to design and implement a strategy for you, but the key to success still will be you. And you—and anyone you hire—must be keenly aware of the unique issues involved in the home inspection business. Keep in mind that most inspections are requested by people buying a house. Chances are good that you will never have even met them before you arrive to inspect the house they want to buy. They may have gotten your name from a real estate agent, from a friend, out of the phone book, or from the Internet. Most of them won't spend a lot of time finding you because they are under tremendous time pressure to get the house inspected so they can finalize a contract.

And they are probably going to live in that house for awhile, so they won't need you again for some time. But don't forget that the person selling the house might be buying another one to move into, and that new dwelling is likely to need inspecting. Doing a good job for the buyer—relaying your findings in a professional, forthright, and unemotional manner—is likely to also impress the seller and the real estate agents involved in the deal. You want them to notice and request you when it comes time to inspect another house.

And never, *never* discount the influence of a satisfied buyer/ client on his universe of friends, family, and co-workers.

> "Home inspection is no different from any other profession. You do the best job possible. Happy clients become your sales force. For me, it's my past 7,000 clients," says Dennis Robitaille of Able Home Inspection in Saugus, Massachusetts. ∎

As you can imagine, it takes a while to get there.

"It's a tough business to get into initially," Dennis Robitaille concedes. "The majority of inspectors when they first became home inspectors went to real estate agencies and talked to them, gave them brochures. It's a waste of time. A new inspector really has to go several months without a paycheck.

"They have to learn how to do hard marketing," says Robitaille.

Robitaille, an inspector since 1982 and in a state that now forbids real estate agents from referring inspectors, says he used various techniques to build his business.

"If there's an open house, I would send a letter to the person selling the house because I knew they were going to be in the market somewhere else. Another technique is to drive down the street and if you see a chimney that's got bricks falling off, or something else about the house that's wrong, is to drop them a letter that says, 'Hi. I was driving down your street and I couldn't help but notice you might have a problem.'

"Other ways of building up PR are to write articles and send newsletters to attorneys and other professionals."

These techniques work, whether you are part of a franchise or on your own.

Remember, the number one thing you want your marketing to convey is that you are a competent professional.

Never announce yourself as a new home inspector or reveal that you are opening a new business. Instead, find ways to show off your expertise. To reach consumers, you could contact your local adult education program and propose to teach classes on how a home works or how to check major components for problems. Organizers of adult education programs are often interested in learning about new ideas for classes that will be beneficial for the community. *Look at it this way*: If you offer people an overview of one of their most valuable possessions, they may turn to you for a more extensive look.

Another idea: Contact local real estate agents, realty firms, and banks to offer to conduct a presentation on home inspection at a new homebuyers seminar they may be planning to offer. These seminars are a common way for real estate agents and banks to market themselves. Be part of their marketing efforts and you'll gain exposure with them and to consumers.

Diane Marotz of Madison, Wisconsin, says she's found business by looking beyond the traditional inspections done prior to home purchases. She writes articles for a women's magazine in her state, touting the benefits of presale inspections and emphasizing that there's "an advantage to a seller knowing what's going on before trying to sell the property." Another avenue, she says, is letting people know that inspectors can help them learn more about their homes.

"I got a call from a woman who lived in a house and who had lost her husband. She realized she didn't know beans about what was going on with the house. She needed someone to come in and go through the house completely with her and give her an objective opinion," says Marotz. "That way we could do some problem solving and look at the whole picture."

The Basics

Before you start thinking about all the innovative ways to sell yourself and all the services you can offer beyond the traditional inspection (see Chapter 20 for more on that), let's start with some basic marketing tools you'll need to get started.

Your company name. It goes without saying that you should choose a name that is unlike any other home inspection company names in your area. Pick one that's easy to remember and makes the kind of impression you want. Your company name is your most visible marketing tool.

A slogan/motto. If you decide to adopt one or use one from your organization or franchise, make sure it is part of all of your marketing materials and advertisements. Put yourself in the shoes of your client and think: WIIFM—What's in it for me? That's what your clients want to know. What will they gain by hiring you? Develop your slogan accordingly. Make it short enough that people will remember it and it can fit on your business card and other materials.

Business cards. These are essential. You will be handing these out whenever you can and to whomever you meet, inside and outside the real estate transaction. Some people believe you always should hand out two cards at a time—one for them to keep and the other for them to pass along to someone else.

And for those who received that passed-on card (from a trusted friend, no less), it will provide their first impression of you. Make it count.

You have several options for obtaining business cards. You can go to your local printing company to develop them, from start to finish. If you are computer-literate, you can go to the Internet and type in "free business cards" in your Internet search feature and you'll find companies that will give you 250 cards for only the cost of shipping and handling (although they would prefer to sell you a more advanced version that costs more). And if you're very technosavvy, your local office supply store most likely will carry business card paper that includes directions on how to make your own business cards from your computer.

What should your business cards say? Remember, they are a marketing tool. Don't waste an opportunity to sell yourself through your business cards. Obviously, they should have your company name, slogan, your name, your location or inspection geographic area (e.g., "Serving the Atlanta metropolitan area"), and at least one business telephone number.

Should you provide an 800 number? Some inspectors say definitely not and that people feel more comfortable with a local inspector they believe knows their area. But what if you bought a franchise? The words "locally owned and operated" will work for you, too.

Here are some of the acronyms and designations that you might see on a home inspector's business card:

AII	Member of the American Institute of Inspectors, Associate Membership open to anyone paying the fee but Certified Membership requires passage of AII training program or another recognized certification exam.
AII Certified Member	Member of the American Institute of Inspectors, Associate Membership open to anyone paying the fee but Certified Membership requires passage of AII training program or another recognized certification exam.
AIS	Member of the American Inspectors Society after passing its training program.
ASHI®	Member of the American Society of Home Inspectors and the logo can only be used by meeting certain qualifications. Three levels of membership—Candidate, Candidate with Logo, and Full. Candidate with Logo and Full must take an exam and have inspection reports verified. All levels require continuing education. *www.ashi.org*
Certified Home Inspector™	Certified by the American Association of Home Inspectors, AAHI™. Must complete 90 hours of inspection education or have three years of experience, plus pass a written exam.
CHI	Certified Home Inspector designation, requiring passage of 100-question open-book exam, offered by the Housing Inspection Foundation.
CRI	Certified Real Estate Inspector designation offered by the National Association of Home Inspectors. Must pass one of three nationally recognized exams, complete 250 fee-paid inspections and then pass a CRI test. Annual review and continuing education required.

FIHI®	Member of Foundation for Independent Home Inspection, no test but must promise not to be influenced by others.
HBIA	Member of the Historic Building Inspectors Association, must pass a standardized exam, complete 200 fee-paid inspections and submit two reports on pre-1925 buildings.
HIF	Member of the Housing Inspection Foundation that offers RHI to those with two years of experience, or 50 inspections, and CHI to those completing 50 inspections and 100-question open book test.
IHINA	Member of Independent Home Inspectors of North America, no exam but must pledge not to solicit leads from real estate agents.
NABIE	Member of the National Academy of Building Inspection Engineers, state-licensed professional engineers and registered architects only.
NACHI	Member of the National Association of Certified Home Inspectors. Must pass three online tests for Associate level. Must participate in 100 inspections, take continuing ed and retake test annually for full membership.
NAHI	Member of the National Association of Home Inspectors, two levels of membership plus CRI (Certified Real Estate Inspector) designation available. Continuing education required for all and annual review for CRI.
NARIES™	Member of National Association of Real-estate Inspection & Evaluation Services, open to anyone associated with the ARIES™ training program.

NIBI® Certified Inspector	Certification offered by the National Institute of Building Inspectors to those who have completed NIBI® training or passed the National Home Inspectors Exam, completed at least 50 home inspections and must carry Errors & Omissions insurance plus go through annual recertification.
RHI	Registered Home Inspector designation for those with two years of experience or 50 home inspections, offered by the Housing Inspection Foundation.
SPREI	The Society of Professional Real Estate Inspectors, no experience required.

The telephone number should be one where someone calling for an appointment will be able to quickly get an answer on when it can be scheduled. The first preference would be a live person answering by stating the company name (and preferably not you, who should be out in the field working). This could be a live person in your office who can schedule an appointment, or an answering service that could page you. (Remember: you don't want clients calling a number that is busy because your teenager is chatting with friends for hours at a time.)

There also is the option of voice mail or an answering machine—but some people will hang up and call someone else because they don't want to wait for your return call. Therefore, your message should request that callers leave a message unless they need to schedule an appointment, and in that case, they should call your cell phone number (and you should provide it, slowly and distinctly).

Or you could have your office number forwarded to your cell phone. But what if they call your cell phone number and you are in the middle of an inspection? Some inspectors say this can be OK if you tell a client ahead of time that you have your cell phone on because you pride yourself on your accessibility but if you are required to take a call, you will do so quickly and get back to the inspection at hand because their inspection is your first priority. Rather than be annoyed by the calls, they may be impressed that they have hired a very sought-after inspector. But if they are annoyed, by all means—*turn off the cell phone.*

When you receive a call on your cell phone while you are working, try to quickly establish the reason for the call. If the caller wants to schedule an inspection, do it then. But add that you are in the middle of an inspection and will return their call within an hour (or however much time you think you need) to discuss their request further if they wish.

What about putting your cell phone number on your business card? That's a choice you have to make. It does make you appear accessible. However, be aware that people who do not need an immediate answer or want to schedule an appointment may call your cell phone first and interrupt your work.

Be sure your business card includes a business e-mail address and the address of your Web site (more on this below).

Are you licensed? Say so on the card. Have you passed a national or state test? Say so.

Are you a member of a local or national home inspector organization? Say so. Have you passed the group's test or received a certification or designation of some type from the group(s)? Say so. Most groups also allow you to use their logo on your promotional materials.

However, if you belong to a group that has so far granted you only "associate" or "candidate" membership, consider not including those words if possible. The fact that you are not a full member will tell people you are new (even if it's only to that organization) and they may also interpret that to mean "less experienced."

E-mail address. Whether you like it or not, the number of people using the Internet to research the various parts of the real estate transaction continues to grow by leaps and bounds. That means these people, your potential clients, are comfortable (and may prefer) using e-mail to do business. They will want the opportunity to be able to e-mail you to set up an appointment, ask questions, or inquire about the results of your report. Neither you nor they want such inquiries to be made in a telephone call at 4 A.M. or any other odd hour when the buyer may be thinking about the home inspection. They consider it more courteous and efficient to reach you by e-mail. But you have to read—and respond to—e-mail every day. If you do not, they will find someone who will.

Because potential clients will probably prefer that you be out doing inspections during the day rather than sitting by your computer, consider an e-mail "automatic response" that says something like this: "Thank you for your e-mail. Today is (insert date) and I will be out of the office doing inspections for most of the day. To schedule an appointment, please call (give the number where a human voice will answer). If you have questions about the services I offer, my Web site is www.(your site).com. Otherwise, I will respond to your e-mail when I return to my office (and give the time you expect to return)."

If you are using a laptop computer on-site and have access to the Internet, check your e-mail messages when you can.

A few more words about e-mail:

- Don't send e-mail to anyone you don't have a working relationship with. People get angry if you send them unsolicited e-mail, which is commonly called "spam" and is considered the junk mail of the Internet.
- Don't "attach" anything (including your report) to an e-mail unless you have told the person on the receiving end beforehand that you will be doing so. Attachments such as photos and forms can take a great deal of time for someone else to download into their computer. The person on the receiving end may think you are sending them spam, or may be concerned about getting a computer virus, and delete the message rather than download the file.
- Be sure to include all the communication basics on every business e-mail you send: your name, company name, e-mail address, and a telephone number. Some e-mail services allow you to store this "signature" so that it can be reused each time.

And finally, use a professional e-mail address. The best option is to have an e-mail address connected to your business Web site with your company's name. If you do not, at least use an address with your name or your new profession in it. For example, *Tim-Cook@yourInternetprovider.com* or *FirstInspections@yourInternetprovider.com*. How serious should anyone take you if your e-mail address is something like *"ILikeFood2@yourInternetprovider.com"* or *"MoviesRule@yourInternetprovider.com"*?

Web site. You need to be listed on the Internet. Period. Even if you know nothing about computers (though you'd better learn if you want to keep up with your competition in this business), you still need to be on the Internet. You can do this through a listing in a national or state organization's online directory of home inspectors or via your franchise's directory.

But the best thing you can do for yourself, and to convey the impression that you are a professional comfortable with technology (and right or wrong, your clients want to believe technology is part of what home inspectors do), is to have a business Web site.

This site should have your business name as its domain name, as in *www.topinspectors.com*. (Your e-mail address could then become something like: *Fred@topinspectors.com* or *FredFox@topinspectors.com*.) You will have to "buy" your domain name. You can go to sites like *http://InternetCrusade.com* or *www.Internic.net* to see if the domain name you want is owned by someone else. If not, then register the name for a year for about $50, and maybe even less, on those sites.

Your Web site doesn't have to be dramatic or do a lot. It should include much of the same information you are going to put into your brochure (see below). Again, if you aren't on the Internet, people may look for someone who is.

Your investment in a Web site will not be huge and it will be worth it, particularly in the years to come, because use of the Internet is only going to increase. And you will have to be part of it if you are going to stay in business over the long term.

Don't let this scare you. Think of your Web site as your business card to the world. It becomes the place people go to learn about you and also to find you if they've lost your paper business card.

There are many knowledgeable folks who can quickly set up a simple, fully functional Web site that provides your contact information, lists your expertise and services, and gives people reasons to hire you. It doesn't even have to be updated regularly unless you want it to be. You may be lucky enough to have a friend or a computer-savvy child who can create your Web site. There are also fairly simple software programs today that even can walk you through the process of setting one up by yourself. You may need to do a little research to find what will work best for you. Home inspector organizations often can steer you toward recommended programs and you also can check with your local computer software store for additional advice.

If you find you want to do it yourself, the Microsoft company offers a couple of Web site development software tools, such as FrontPage and Microsoft Publisher, that are pretty easy to learn. Also, the Adobe software company has a family of Web design products like GoLive and others that really are for the novice Web designer. You can download these programs from either Microsoft or Adobe, or buy them at local software stores. Retail, the programs typically cost a couple of hundred dollars—unless you add on a number of bells and whistles, making the price substantially higher. (You can easily spend more than $1,000 on Web software if you really want your site to do tricks.)

If you look around a little, you can often find software on sale—but don't expect a big break. And whatever you do, if you have a brand-new computer, do not buy five-year-old software to run on it. System compatibility is crucial.

For those of you who are a little less nerdy, there are technology companies out there that have developed Web site templates and Web hosting specifically for the home inspection business. Two of the good ones can be found at *alamode.com* and *home-inspect.com*. For around $400 or so per year, these people will help you buy the domain name you want, provide you with a handful of e-mail addresses, host your site on the Internet, and provide you with a means to update your site at will.

Obviously, your name and address and other information are plugged into their templates. But they also offer opportunities for consumers to order inspections on line, order ancillary services, read testimonials about you, and basically let the Web surfers of the world know you're good at what you do.

For the non-nerd, these companies can make you look very good for comparatively little money. But if you need to hire a professional, first take a look at the Web sites of other inspectors in your area. At the very bottom of the opening page, you may find the name of the company that created the site. Once you find some Web sites that you like, contact those companies that created them. Or ask other businesspeople you know who they hired for their Web sites and why.

You will need a Web site hosting company, but you can find those in the phone book or by searching the Internet, or your local Internet provider may even offer that service. For a monthly or annual fee, this company will make sure your site remains in cyberspace.

Brochures. This is a major marketing tool for you. You will be sending them to real estate agents and mortgage brokers and bankers. You will be giving them to buyers and to sellers. You should leave them at every house you inspect. You must try to get them into the hands of everyone you want to do business with—and their friends.

Don't go cheap.

A cheap-looking, amateur flyer will make you look like a struggling, unprofessional newcomer who doesn't have the expertise or time to do it right. Why would anyone want to hire someone like that?

This doesn't mean you have to go out and hire a marketing firm. But it does mean you have to invest a little money in quality paper and a little time in getting the words right. And that means spelled correctly, too. Every computer has a "spellcheck" function. Use it. And then ask two or three people whom you consider to have more than a passing familiarity with correct grammar, punctuation, and usage to review the words you want to put on the quality paper. Remember, spellcheck won't distinguish between the right word and a wrong one if both are spelled correctly.

The brochure should fit into a standard No. 10 envelope, so it can be mailed. (Use stamps rather than a postage meter so the mailing looks more personal.) Make sure the brochure's ink is dark enough that it can be easily copied (real estate agents may want to make copies for clients, etc.). Use only one or two different styles of print fonts and either no, or very few, words in all capital letters; otherwise, it will be too difficult to read and distracting. Don't use weird ink or paper colors. Leave some "white space" around the text of your brochure so it's easier to read. Use heavier paper or high-gloss paper, even if printing with your own computer and printer. Think quality.

People want personal service, professionalism, and benefits. They don't want a difficult experience. They don't care much about what your company can do for them. They want to know what you, the inspector, will do for them. Keep these things in mind when developing your brochure.

Here are some additional critical elements to consider for the content of any brochure:

Business basics. Always put your company name, slogan, your name, business telephone number, e-mail address, and Web site address where people can easily find them. Put your business name, or your name if you don't have a business name, in a prominent position on the top of the front page.

Pictures. Put your picture in the brochure. You are selling yourself. You want those reading your brochure to want to hire you as their inspector.

But make sure your picture is flattering. You don't want to look scary, dirty, or like an escaped criminal. Don't look like someone they'd be reluctant to let into the house. You also don't want to appear too young, too old, or too fat to do the job.

You should look neat and professional. But you don't want to seem too dressed up to inspect someone's attic or basement, so forget the tie. On the other hand, a T-shirt could make you look like a worker instead of an inspector. A clean shirt with a collar is a good bet. One that is monogrammed with your business name is better.

What other pictures should you include? You want the picture(s) to help sell your services. Don't just include a picture of a house. It takes up valuable space, and what message does it convey? Instead, you might include a picture of you doing an inspection or using a certain gauge. Don't forget the caption! It shouldn't say "Me using a gauge." Better to use wording such as "I use the latest technology to give you the most accurate results."

You also might consider including a picture of the type of report you will provide, possibly including the binder cover and some open pages. Again, the caption shouldn't be "My report." Consider instead: "My 500-point report provides you with a detailed assessment."

Some also say cartoons are a no-no. You want to make an impression as a serious professional. Any illustrations and pictures you use should support that view.

Your qualifications. As with your business cards, you want to list if you are licensed (and the license number), what examinations you have passed, what groups you belong to (remember to state in your brochure that you are a "member in good standing"), and what designations or certifications you have earned. If you have started the local chapter of a state or national group or have been elected to office, say so. If you have taken a special home inspection course, include that. If you follow a group's standards of practice, state that information.

Here's where you also can list things like the following: available seven days a week, appointments scheduled anytime between 7 A.M. and 10 P.M., service provided in the tri-state area, final report provided on-site, available for follow-up questions, I'll give you a thorough, easy-to-read report, etc. If you have errors and omissions insurance, you might want to tout that (or perhaps not; see Chapter 15). It shows you are responsible and professional.

Testimonials. Prospective clients want to read the glowing words of your satisfied customers. When you hear some, ask if you can use them in your brochures. Never do it without the person's permission. You should include a positive quotation, along with the person's name and town. Consider putting this information in italics or a separate box so it stands out.

Your services. This is where you list what you can offer your clients. Remember WIIFM? (What's in it for me?) You needn't waste space telling them why they should hire a home inspector. They wouldn't be reading your brochure if they didn't already know. Instead, give them reasons to hire *you.*

List some of the highlights of your traditional home inspection. "You get a 500-point inspection, including a thorough examination of: roofs, vents," and so on. Consider including "maintenance tips" and ending with "and much more."

Be sure to list any optional services you can provide, such as presale inspections. (See Chapter 20 for some more ideas.) If you are trained to offer inspections in other areas, such as radon, septic systems, water quality, or wood infestation, make sure to list these services.

If you are not, consider finding people in your area who are and then working out a subcontracting arrangement. Someone reading your brochure would see something like "Wood infestation inspections available for an additional fee and performed by a certified inspector, License No. xxxx." That way, the business comes through you. Remember, people want things to be easy.

Your prices. You may want to say "Personal quote available on request" or "Call for a price sheet" if you prefer to work that way. But some people are going to want the answer before they even call you. Keep in mind that those same people may not even know whether your price is reasonable or not. They just want to see some straightforward figures. If you don't list them or use extremely complicated price structures, they may think you are trying to put something over on them. Better to list your prices per square foot, or by age, or whatever formula you have decided to use. (See Chapter 9 for more.)

Remember, you are using this brochure to tell them why they should hire you. You want them to believe that you are the best home inspector in town. Don't list extremely low prices or they will think you are a cut-rate inspector. Better to charge above the going rate because you're worth it.

Also, including discount coupons as part of your brochure can be self-defeating. First, no one wants to have to cut a coupon out of your brochure (and the brochure will get thrown away rather than passed on if there's a big hole in the middle of it). Second, your brochure might give the impression that you are a cut-rate inspector—that you will work for less. You want them to see you as a respected professional. If you decide to try discount coupons, offer them separately from your brochure.

Your vehicle. You are in business. Put your name on your vehicle, either permanently or with a magnetic sign. Every time someone sees your vehicle at a house, they will think you are doing an inspection. Every time they see it drive by, they will believe you are on your way to an inspection. They'll think that if you are so busy, you must be really good. If you don't have a lot of business yet, go drive around in your vehicle to gain visibility and to look for houses for sale so you can send your brochure to the sellers.

Your shirt. That's right. Every time you wear a shirt (preferably polo style) with your name or company name on it, you are a walking marketing tool, both on the job and off. Don't be afraid to use a somewhat more unusual color here, especially if it's the same color as your vehicle or the lettering on the sign on your vehicle. You are trying to distinguish yourself from every other inspector. Your shirt is another way to do that, but don't go crazy the other way and leave a less than professional impression.

Your report. Your inspection report will be seen by people beyond your client. While you should put a picture and the address of the home you are inspecting on the cover, don't forget your company name and contact information. Your report should look professional and be easy to understand. It may be helpful to include maintenance tips for the homeowner, which means your report will be kept on the shelf for handy accessibility—and also readily available for reference when someone asks your clients for the name of their home inspector. Consider also including your brochure and the list of standards of practice you follow, along with more extensive contact information. Some inspectors provide three-ring binders for their reports, and may also include home reference manuals and other prepared materials that may be of specific interest to a particular client.

Who Can You Market To?

Real estate agents. In most states, real estate agents are key to your success. Although regulations vary by state, in most cases it will be the real estate agent that a buyer will turn to for advice when it comes time to schedule a home inspection. They may be prevented by law or company policy from recommending a specific inspector. But that may not prevent them from steering their client away from a bad one.

Again, real estate agents want a competent inspector who will do a thorough job (protecting them from being sued by an angry buyer) without killing a deal. This means you will be expected to be professional and to report your findings in a professional manner, along with any advice you have for solving any problems you may find.

But some real estate agents have been using the same home inspectors for years. Getting your name on their lists isn't as simple as calling up agents and asking to be added.

Alyssa Hickson of National Home Inspection of Malabar, Florida, said what has surprised her most about the home inspection business is "how difficult it is to get your foot into the door of some real estate offices."

"It surprised me how some people continue to stick with who they have been working with and the lengths you have to go to get someone to try you out. I have had to offer a free home inspection just to get someone to try me out. They are so leery of a bad inspection and so afraid of losing a sale."

Hickson says her outreach efforts to real estate agents have included providing coupons for free inspections and sample packets that include information on her inspection reports, along with a pen with her name and phone number on it. Her agent "goodie bags" also may include measuring tapes and levels (again with the company name on them).

Think about an item real estate agents would find useful that you can put your name on, so when it comes time for them to suggest an inspector, your name is easy to find.

Do not offer them kickbacks or referral fees. This can call into question impartiality and ethics.

If you do decide to offer discount coupons for an agent to give to clients, that agent probably will be more comfortable doing so if the coupon clearly states that the coupon does not represent an endorsement by the agent but is being passed on as a courtesy.

Some inspectors believe the best way to prove your capabilities to a real estate agent is to offer to do a free seller's prelisting inspection. The listing agent and his or her clients are likely to appreciate knowing ahead of time what a buyer's inspection could reveal. That way they can either fix any problems that are discovered or be prepared to explain them. This advance knowledge will prove valuable in any negotiations. Your work during the seller's inspection (which is becoming more popular, by the way) will provide an opportunity for the agent to see your work and how you communicate your findings, both verbally and in your written report.

Another possibility is to ask to make a presentation to a real estate agency's sales meeting. Bring your brochures, business cards, a sample report—and food. Most sales meetings are held in the mornings, so bring breakfast-type foods: bagels, pastries, coffee cake, fresh fruit. Coffee is likely to be already available, but you might consider offering juices. Bring nice paper products and/or napkins, along with eating utensils and plastic cups if appropriate.

What should your presentation involve, beyond getting your name and face in front of the agents? It should showcase your expertise. One topic that could be useful to agents is a reminder on how to easily prepare a house for inspection (to save both you and the agent time). You would remind them to make sure all areas are accessible, keys are handy if something needs to be unlocked, and so on. Or, you might talk about the benefits of prelisting inspections. Sometimes you can get the ball rolling by asking if they have ever had a negative experience with a home inspector or if they have any questions about the home inspection process.

Mortgage bankers. Introduce yourself and drop off brochures to local mortgage bankers. Sometimes potential buyers will seek to be preapproved for a mortgage before they ever start looking for a house or contact a real estate agent. Those people will want a home inspection done somewhere down the line. It would be nice if they already had your brochure.

Real estate attorneys. The attorney is often another player in the real estate transaction. If a real estate contract comes before an attorney and hasn't included an inspection, he or she might suggest it would be wise to have the house inspected anyway. And the attorney might just happen to have your brochure handy.

Sellers. As we've already said, sellers can be a good source of business for you. Send them your brochure, business cards, and a note to the effect that you notice they are selling their home and perhaps they would be interested in a seller's inspection or an inspection of their next home. Note: You may want to develop a brochure just for this market.

Any homeowner. An inspection can help people learn more about their homes and the maintenance they should be doing. Many people today do not have the skills to understand how their home works. You can offer them an expert's tour of their own home, along with advice on any steps they could take to make sure their house is safe and in good shape.

Also, in some states, a professional inspection of some type may be necessary or desired in order to obtain, or maintain, homeowner's insurance, particularly in waterfront areas.

But again, the only way for any of these potential markets to find you is for you to market to them.

CHAPTER 7

Where Do You Fit in the Deal?

What happened before you got to the house and what's going to happen after you leave?

As a home inspector, it's a good idea for you to understand where you fit into the "Big Picture" of the real estate transaction. It's also a good idea to have some insight into how those "other" people—the real estate agents, appraisers, bankers, title people, lawyers—fit in as well.

Make no mistake: Understanding what's gone on between the various parties before you got to the house will not make you better at checking the mechanics of the home. Nor, after you leave, is anything that happens between them likely to have any impact on whether the roof does or doesn't leak.

Your job remains clear: to inspect the house.

But understanding how a transaction comes together will help you sympathize, and empathize, with what your clients are going through. People-wise, these are the kinds of things that make you a better home inspector, which leads to repeat business and referrals. It's one thing to understand the profession—it's another to understand the business.

As we've emphasized before (and will throughout this book), whether you realize it or not, as a home inspector you are a pivotal person in the deal. What you find or don't find in the house may very well decide whether the transaction lives or dies. Your report could swing the price of a home by thousands, or even tens of thousands, of dollars.

Even worse, if you find something the seller didn't feel obligated to disclose, tempers could flare and the whole deal could blow up. On the other hand, if your report comes in the way everyone hopes, it could trigger big smiles all around, followed by firm handshakes and pats on the back.

(Of course, the funny thing is, you may never actually know how it all comes out.)

When Does the Process Begin?

By most estimates, the typical real estate transaction truly begins sometime around New Year's and culminates sometime around May or June.

Right around the holidays is when most families begin looking around their current dwelling and begin shaking their collective heads. "We just can't live here another year," they begin to believe, for whatever reason. Whether they realize it or not, at that moment they have begun their search for a new home.

Over the next few weeks they'll be talking to friends and relatives. "What do you think about this house?" or "that neighborhood?" "Do you know a good real estate agent?" "Do you know where to get a loan?"

At this point, you—the inspector—are not even a twinkle in the homebuyer's eye. They are nowhere near ready to think about potential problems with a home they haven't even seen yet.

By early February, those who are going to buy houses decide it's time to get serious. About 90 percent of the time, "getting serious" means they start to look at houses on the Internet, pick up the weekend newspaper, or peruse those small home-advertising magazines at supermarkets and restaurants.

Also about now, most of them are starting to take a hard look at their finances and beginning to stockpile cash. These are spooky times. The rule of thumb is they don't think they have enough money to really do what they'd like.

Nevertheless, somewhere around mid-March, most serious homebuyers start doing a couple of interesting things: They drive around neighborhoods trying to get an idea of what's for sale. And they will probably start going to "Open Houses."

Also, about this time is when they hire a real estate agent. What kind of agent they find may determine whether you—the inspector—get hired some weeks from now. It could even set the parameters of your inspection.

Real Estate Agents

So let's talk about real estate agents for just a few seconds (more about them in Chapter 8). In fact, there are all kinds of real estate agents these days, and it's worth your while to know which ones are which. Later in this chapter, we'll go over "how to read" a business card, but for the moment, generally the people you will be dealing with are described below.

Buyer agents. A real estate agent who describes himself or herself as a "buyer's agent" is expected to have the best interest of the homebuyer at heart. He or she is the same as you, probably under contract to represent the buyer's interest. Usually a buyer's agent wants you to do a thorough job on behalf of your mutual client. You and a good buyer agent are allies. This agent usually will be on the property, or nearby, to make sure the buyers won't overreact to what you find.

Listing agent. In your travels you may also run into a "listing agent" who is helping (but not legally tied to) a buyer who is interested in a specific home. The listing agent is the one who is hired by the seller to sell the house you are inspecting. Because the listing agent legally represents the seller, and therefore is trying to get the seller the best possible deal, the listing agent may be less enthusiastic about seeing you. Many listing agents see you as the person who is going to punch a hole in the seller's asking price. They believe you are the one who is going to force their seller to reduce the price. (In reality, the listing agent should be glad to see you do a thorough job. Defects that are brought to light in an inspection are infinitely better than defects brought to light later in a lawsuit. It's really better for everyone to get things out in the open early.)

Facilitator. In theory, at least, a facilitator is a real estate nonagent, legally bound to neither the buyer nor seller. He or she has no vested interest in whether the price holds up or not. The facilitator is merely involved in the deal to help the two sides talk to each other. Again, he or she may or may not be at the inspection. In theory, whatever you find should be fine with a facilitator. As a practical matter, however, don't be surprised to see facilitators (inappropriately) act as advocates for the seller. Like all agents, they don't get paid unless the deal closes. They don't want your inspection to jeopardize their income.

Transaction broker. Basically, a transaction broker has the same duties as a facilitator.

Fee-for-service agent. This is a new breed of agent, one who does only specific tasks for a specific fee. These agents may be hired only to show properties, not to negotiate deals. Or they may be hired only to fill out the paperwork after the buyers have found the house and negotiated their own deal.

One of the more important things for you to remember is that with the exception of the fee-for-service agent, the real estate agents don't get paid unless the deal closes.

How can you find out what kind of agent you're dealing with? Ask the agent or ask your client. You'll be amazed at how your attitude will change depending on the answer. If the buyers are working with a buyer agent, then odds are the agent is looking out after the interest of the client. If the only other professional in the deal is the listing agent, then you are the buyer's primary source of protection and only true ally. Likewise, if it's a facilitator or transaction broker, you may be your client's only defense. And if the client is working with a fee-for-service agent, well, you're just going to have to ask what his or her role is in the deal.

Speaking of which ...

Back to the Deal

Once the consumers have selected a real estate agent to help them, that agent probably is going to recommend that the buyer get prequalified for a mortgage. (A prequalification letter is a statement from a lender that tells the buyer how much he or she can borrow.) That, of course, is the role of the mortgage broker or mortgage banker. Some buyers will wait until after they have found the house.

In the course of your inspection, odds are you will never meet the lender. The lender, however, will be interested in your work. The lender, after all, wants to make sure that the buyer not only can make the payments, but also can afford the upkeep on the house. If your report recommends a new $5,000 roof, some lenders are going to take that into consideration when they decide on the loan (except for the Federal Housing Administration, which requires that a roof must last for the next two years).

So again, you may not be aware of the mortgage lender, but the lender probably is aware of you.

After the buyer, the agent, and the lender are all on the same page In terms of how much the buyer can afford, the buyer can then get serious about looking at houses.

According to research by the National Association of REALTORS®, most homebuyers today spend about six weeks in the actual looking-for-a-house phase: the first couple of weeks on their own and then using an agent in the last few weeks to help them really focus in on what they want.

It is not unusual for homebuyers to look at—which is to say, physically walk through—six or seven homes before deciding on one. It also is not unusual for them to view as many as 20 homes. (You hear horror stories from agents about people visiting as many as 50 homes over a period of months. Most agents consider those people a waste of their time.)

So somewhere around late April or early May, homebuyers likely have found a house they think their family will like.

The buyers probably see the house once on a tour of homes, spend about 15 minutes inside it, and then put it on a "keeper" list as they move on to see other properties.

Later, the buyers and their agents review that "keeper" list and decide to revisit one or two. Again, however, they'll probably only spend 20 minutes or so inside the house and walking around outside. They are being somewhat more critical and are trying to see things they may have missed before.

Finally, they settle on the one they want.

From there, assuming they are working with a buyer agent, their agent contacts the listing agent and negotiations begin.

The buyers make an offer, giving the seller 24 or 48 hours or so to respond. The offer represents the first time that you—the home inspector—are officially mentioned. In fact, you are a key point in the negotiating strategy. You are a contingency clause that simply states the buyers may not go forward with the deal unless they are satisfied with your report. (And they haven't even hired you yet.) If it's a seller's market—with many buyers wanting the same house—the inspection contingency could be jettisoned altogether to win the house.

However, the seller usually makes a counteroffer and may even make an attempt to eliminate the inspection from the contract. With luck, however, the buyers (with the advice of the buyer agent) stick to their guns and say nothing is going to happen until you've looked over the property.

Hopefully, the seller sees the light and agrees to allow an inspection—but only if it can be done in the next ten days or less (depending on what's been negotiated).

That's your cue.

You go out, and for the next two to three hours, inspect the house and write up the report. You hand the report to the buyer with one hand as you accept a check, Visa/MasterCard, or cash with the other hand, and then you leave. Now, you may consider this a job well done!

After you leave, however, the real estate negotiating process may very well begin again, depending on what's in the report.

> Samuel Wood, a professional civil engineer from South Charleston, West Virginia, says he recommends that the price of repairs be agreed upon by the buyer and seller, and then have the homebuyer contract for the work, "so that they have quality control over the repairs. That also prevents 'compliance inspections' later that are always a lose-lose situation. They rarely pass." ■

The buyers and their agent may note your remarks that the roof is near the end of its life span and ask the sellers to reduce their price by $5,000. They may note that the hot water temperature is a little disappointing, and ask for a new water heater.

And it goes on and on, until everything in your report is reconciled one way or another.

Samuel Wood notes when the seller arranges for the repairs, they usually don't get done until the day before closing. Then the inspector comes back in, sees the job isn't done right, and reports it back to the buyer, who then refuses to close. "Who do they blame?" asks Wood.

Yes, the home inspector—for finding the defects and delaying the closing. For example, a typical inspection might pick up on a lightning strike that has damaged wiring coming into the house, but that inspection might not trace the strike all the way to a damaged fuse box inside the house.

"If the homeseller is in charge of repairs, he's going to stop the work when the damage is repaired outside. But if the buyer is responsible for hiring the electrician, that electrician is going to know to check for additional damage and make sure the job is done right," offers Wood.

After that, the buyers go back to their lender and make sure everything is OK on the mortgage end of things. The lender immediately hires another member of the transaction process, the appraiser, to go out to take a look at the property from a different perspective.

The appraiser is there to make sure the house is worth what the seller says it's worth and what the buyers have agreed to pay for it. The appraiser is not going to comb through the house like you did. In fact, the appraiser's "inspection" starts with public records to determine whether other homes in the neighborhood that are of similar size and style have sold for roughly the same amount as your buyer is prepared to pay.

If the appraiser does not believe the house is worth the money, the bank will not loan the full amount.

There are occasions when you and the appraiser will be at the property at the same time, usually by coincidence. It always pays to be friendly, and certainly an exchange of business cards is appropriate. But keep in mind that your client is the buyers, and the appraiser's client is the bank. There is no reason for an appraiser to receive your report prior to your client. The bank will probably want a copy of your report as well, but that's really up to the buyers—not you.

As the deal is struck, the buyers also usually check in with a lawyer to make sure the sales contracts are everything they need to be.

It would be rare for you to ever talk to a client's lawyer, but again, it's not impossible that he would want you to clarify a finding. Just be sure to keep your remarks specific to the question. If he asks about something you didn't inspect, say so.

About this time, the buyers also are making contact with a title company. The title company's job is literally to make sure the seller has the right to sell the house. The title company makes sure there are no long-divorced spouses lurking with names still on the title and/or that there are no liens on the house from the last roofer who never got paid by the sellers.

Depending on who the closing officer is—it could be a title company representative, lawyer, or even a lender—that person also is interested in your inspection report. They, however, are only interested in making sure that there was an inspection and that the buyers and seller resolved whatever issues you raised. The closing officer's only interest is that the contingency has been cleared.

Finally, the deal is done, the movers show up with the buyers' furniture, and everyone lives happily ever after.

The key point here, aside from the perspective of where you fit into the transaction, is that even though the home inspection is an extremely important element of the deal, you arrive on the scene very late in the transaction process. For all practical purposes, the buyers have mentally bought the house before you ever see it. And depending on how the contingency is written into the contract, the buyers may not necessarily be able to escape the deal even if you find that the house is a wreck that's about to collapse.

In many contracts, the seller is not obligated to release the buyer from the deal just because the inspection report comes back with issues.

Again, none of this should affect your actual report on the property. It's just important to keep in mind.

How To Read a Business Card

It's a good idea to make a practice of handing out your business card and, in return, collecting other people's business cards. But before you just shove a card into your pocket and move on, take a minute to examine it.

That will help your mind secure the name of the person who gave it to you. But even more important, business cards tell a lot about people and their accomplishments, usually spelled out in those bizarre combinations of initials just after their names. Those letters represent certifications and designations the card owner has received over the years. They usually represent some specialty that has been developed, some education received, or a professional group the bearer decided to join.

Feel free to ask the owner of the card what the initials stand for and how they were received (see chart on page 50). Many times, those initials represent hard work and the person is very proud to discuss them.

A couple of quick, general definitions:

- When someone is *certified* as something, it usually means they have learned a specific skill set that can be applied in a number of different areas. For instance, there are a number of Internet certifications these days that mean the user has learned the various tricks of online communication and can apply them in a number of different ways.

- A *designation,* on the other hand, usually involves specific training for a specific discipline. For instance, there is such a thing in real estate as an ABR, an "Accredited Buyer Representative." That ABR means the broker or agent has learned how to work on problems unique to homebuyers.

Now that you know the difference, you might as well know something else: There are no certification/designation police. You may become involved with people who have "certifications" that sound more like "designations" and vice versa.

Also, some people will keep initials on their business cards long after their designation has expired. Either they saw no need to take them off or didn't want to go to the expense of getting new cards printed.

One more quick note: Why do people get these designations and certifications? Yes, yes, of course, to better serve the consumer. But why else?

Several reasons:

- They are instant credibility. They help convince consumers that they are working with someone who really knows what he or she is doing.
- Professionals like to deal with other professionals who have gone through the same training. For example, if an ASHI member in one state has a client moving to another state, he is going to want to send that client to an ASHI member in the other state.
- Finally, certifications and designations can mean money. According to one survey, for example, real estate agents holding a CRS (Certified Residential Specialist) have an average income of $153,142; those holding the Certified Commercial Investment Member (CCIM) designation make an average of $164,308.

Here is a brief sampling of certifications, designations, and other words that may appear on business cards you would normally see. Most of these have to do with real estate agents and others you may encounter around the property. (Note: Designations and certifications that may appear on a home inspector's business card can be found in Chapter 17.)

> **AAMC** (Accredited Association Management Company)— This is a credential you may see if you are doing an inspection in a condo building or maybe even a property in a homeowner association. The Community Associations Institute gives this certification to professional managers.
>
> **ABR** (Accredited Buyer Representative)—This is a relatively popular and relatively easy-to-get designation offered by the Real Estate Buyer's Agent Council, which is part of the National Association of REALTORS®. The ABR focuses on teaching members how to work with buyers. A lot of attention is paid to helping consumers sidestep legal land mines.
>
> **ABRM** (Accredited Buyer Representative Manager)—This course is mostly for real estate office managers who have a lot of ABRs in their offices.
>
> **AHWD** (At Home with Diversity certification)—This is a rare designation offered jointly by the National Association of REALTORS® and the Department of Housing and Urban Development. It is to help agents be mindful of Fair Housing issues and how to best work with people of varying ethnic backgrounds.
>
> **AMS** (Association Management Specialist)—This is the basic designation given by the Community Associations Institute to those who have learned how to manage homeowner and condo associations.
>
> **CCIM** (Certified Commercial Investment Member)—Some residential real estate agents also have this certification. This is a difficult-to-get certification for those who deal with sales of office buildings, shopping malls, warehouses, and so forth.
>
> **C-CREC** (Certified-Consumer Real Estate Consultant)—The C-CREC is a fairly new certification that is awarded to people who work on a fee-for-service basis. For instance, instead of using a real estate agent for the entire transaction, a buyer might hire a C-CREC to just help negotiate the deal after the buyer found the house.

CEBA (Certified Exclusive Buyer Agent)—This is a rare and fairly rigorous certification course for buyer agents. Many CBEAs never work on the seller side of a deal. They'll work only for homebuyers.

CGA (Certified Graduate Associate)—This is a basic certification for homebuilders that signifies some advanced education in management, sales, and marketing.

CGB (Certified Graduate Builder)—This is an advanced certification for homebuilders that suggests a high level of education in business management, property management, sales, and marketing of new homes.

CIRMS (Community Insurance and Risk Management Specialist)—A designation given by the Community Associations Institute for the study of insurance issues confronting homeowner and condo associations. If you're inspecting a problem property, someone with this designation may be hanging around.

CLHMS (Certified Luxury Home Marketing Specialist)—A certification won by real estate agents who work exclusively in the million-dollar-plus price range. A course is required, plus experience in selling upper-end homes.

CMP (Certified new home Marketing Professional)—The holder of this certification has taken sales training classes in new home sales.

CPM (Certified Property Manager)—A growing number of real estate licensees also become involved in managing rental properties for the owners of those properties. The CPM teaches some of those skills.

CRB (Certified Real Estate Brokerage Manager)—The holder of this certification is usually an office manager who is responsible for the actions of the sales associates on his staff. He may also be actively engaged in working with consumers.

CRE (Counselor of Real Estate)—Another fairly rare certification, CRE holders typically consult on complex commercial or industrial real estate deals, rather than on residential deals.

CRP (Certified Relocation Professional)—This certification helps professionals understand issues involved when a corporation is moving either one employee or many employees. It involves things like coordinating movers and finding new schools for the kids.

CRS (Certified Residential Specialist)—This certification can take years for a real estate agent to earn but is considered one of the best in the real estate business. A CRS has successfully worked with a large number of buyers and sellers and taken extensive marketing courses. It is largely for professionals who work with homesellers, rather than buyers.

CSP (Certified New Home Sales Professional)—A certification given to those who have developed skills in the sales of new homes.

DREI (Distinguished Real Estate Instructor)—This designation is actually for people who teach real estate, but a relative handful of brokers and salespeople around the country also have it. It is very difficult to obtain.

e-PRO (Electronic Real Estate Professional)—This is for real estate agents who have learned to market on the Internet.

GMB (Graduate Master Builder)—One of the highest designations in the homebuilding industry; applicants must have ten years of building experience, already be a CGA, or have an equal certification in the remodeling business.

GRI (Graduate—REALTOR® Institute)—The GRI is actually a very basic how-to-sell real estate course—kind of the equivalent of graduating from Real Estate High School.

LTG (Leadership Training Graduate)—Once fairly popular, this designation is being phased out in lieu of more strenuous real estate management courses.

MCSP (Master Certified New Home Sales Professional)—A more advanced degree of education than required for the CSP.

PCAM (Professional Community Association Manager)—This is earned by individuals who take a special course from the Community Associations Institute.

QSC (Quality Service Certified)—The QSC is offered to agents who are prepared to have consumer feedback about them posted publicly on the Internet.

SIOR (Society of Industrial and Office REALTORS®)—This designation also is fairly rare among residential real estate sales associates.

SRES (Seniors Real Estate Specialist)—This is a relatively new certification gaining popularity inside the real estate industry. Holders of the SRES are trained to work with Baby Boomers and other older people looking at retirement, cashing out of the family home, or who may have other real estate issues on the horizon.

Appraisal Industry

CREA (Certified Real Estate Appraiser)—There are a couple of certifications available to people who are in the appraisal business. This one is offered by the National Association of Real Estate Appraisers. The course reminds appraisers of various factors that can affect the value of properties.

GAA (General Accredited Appraiser)—Another basic appraisal certification, this one is offered by the National Association of REALTORS®, to help professionals understand how to set property values. Extensive coursework and experience are required to obtain the certification, as well as state licensing.

RAA (Residential Accredited Appraiser)—An appraisal course similar to the GAA and also offered by the REALTOR® association. Extensive coursework and experience is required.

Banking Industry

ARO (Accredited Residential Originator)—This is a mortgage industry certification that suggests a high degree of ethics and standards in the origination of residential mortgages.

ARU (Accredited Residential Underwriter)—This is a mortgage certification that can be earned by those who review credit and property applications typically involving one- to four-unit residential properties.

CMB (Certified Mortgage Banker)—This is the basic certification of those who seek a higher level of professionalism in mortgage banking.

CMC (Certified Mortgage Consultant)—Someone who has demonstrated knowledge of the principles and practices of the mortgage profession and laws. Must have at least five years of experience in mortgage finance.

CMT (Certified Mortgage Technologist)—This designation is designed for Information Technology (IT) professionals, managers, and executives in the real estate finance industry. The certification is held by people who understand the impact of technology on mortgage banking.

CRMS (Certified Residential Mortgage Specialist)—A designation that signifies a high level of knowledge and experience in mortgage origination and finance. Holders of the CRMS must have at least two years of experience in mortgage finance or a related field.

One Other Thing

There are, of course, many industry professionals who have no initials behind their names at all. But just because they don't, it doesn't mean they don't meet some level of ethics and proficiency in their field. It more likely means they just don't belong to any of the national organizations that offer the more familiar educational courses.

Designations aren't everything. But they can be regarded as indicators of a willingness to sharpen one's professional skills.

CHAPTER 8

Who Is Your Client?

The guy who writes me a check! Right?
(That is right, isn't it?)

Nothing is ever easy. In this case, it's not really a matter of "What's the right answer?" It's really more a matter of "What's the right question?"

For the record: Who is your client?

Sure, for all practical purposes it's either the guy who hires you or the guy who pays you. Usually those are the same person, and usually it's the buyer. (Though more often, sellers are hiring inspectors for presale inspections.) Usually you can put the "client" name tag on the person who pays you.

The better question, though, is: Who do you represent?

Do you represent your client? *Are you sure?*

There is a growing philosophy in the industry that you don't really represent either the buyer or the seller in the transaction, no matter who pays you, but in fact you represent the "house."

Yes, this is where things get a little dicey.

To review, don't forget that everybody in the transaction has a vested interest in how the home inspection turns out:

- Homebuyers have an agenda. They may *(may)* want you to "find problems" so they can either back out of the deal or get a reduced price. (Or young couples may want you to put a stamp of approval on the house regardless of its shape, because they need to convince Mom and Dad, who may be writing a hefty down payment check, that it's worth the money.)

- Homesellers don't want you to find anything that will jeopardize the deal, and if you do find something, they are going to try to push you to understate the problems.
- Listing agents don't want you to find anything that will keep the deal from going through, but they also don't want you to hide anything that ultimately could get them sued if discovered later. (And it is always discovered later.)
- And buyer agents want to make sure you protect buyers to the max, but without needlessly scaring them away from buying a house that really is right for them.
- And then, there's you. Yes, you also have a vested interest, whether you'll admit it or not. If you get a reputation as a "deal killer," real estate agents are not going to refer their customers to you and in some cases they'll even refuse to work with you—and that could put a serious crimp in your career.

Choose your words wisely. As a new home inspector you are going to find that very few things are black and white. You are going to have to make judgments. And, for sure, every one of those judgments is going to have an impact on the sale, the price, and probably your future.

The Way It Should Be

In Chapter 7 we went over the way real estate transactions come together. Unfortunately, it's not only a relatively honest depiction of how deals happen, but it's also the worst-case scenario.

In a perfect world, the real estate transaction would happen like this:

Mr. and Mrs. Homebuyer would wake up one morning and say to each other, "Gee, honey, I think it's time for us to move out of this apartment and into a home of our own."

From then on, they would exercise due diligence in a number of different categories.

They would be sure to interview three or four real estate agents to find the one most compatible with their agenda. They would interview lenders to learn who was offering the best rates and service. They would talk to several attorneys to decide who would best represent their interests. They would even contact several title insurance companies. (Most consumers don't realize that title insurance is as negotiable as anything else in the transaction.)

And, of course, they would take it upon themselves to contact several different home inspectors. They would interview each of those inspectors, asking each one for prices and credentials. They would be sure to get references from each inspector and, of course, they would actually call those references.

They would ask each inspector about what professional organizations he or she belonged to. They would ask how many inspections the inspectors had conducted in their professional lives, and over what time span. They would ask if the inspector had any special areas of expertise.

The inspector's company's background would be checked out—and, of course, there would be a call to the Better Business Bureau.

The process of just selecting a home inspector would take a couple of weeks. And once they were finished, Mr. and Mrs. Homebuyer would sit down at their dining room table and say something like, "Gee, golly, they were all so nice—but I think I liked Jim best."

In the Real World

In the real world, that kind of diligence happens somewhere around zero percent of the time. And it may actually be less than that.

In the real world, the deal is a pressure cooker and the home inspector is an afterthought.

At best, an inspector isn't contacted until the deal already is in crisis mode. The buyers' purchase agreement already has been accepted, but the sellers are offering them only a ten-day window in which to get the house inspected and resolve any defects that are found.

The buyers are suddenly under pressure to find you, hire you, and get you—the inspector—into the house. The sellers also want to get you in as fast as possible because, let's face it, they need to know if the deal with these buyers is going to work. Realistically, as soon as the sellers accept a purchase agreement, their house moves off the market and into the Twilight Zone. Often, the sellers don't know if the buyers can actually get financing, and the sellers don't know what you, the inspector, are going to come up with that they may have to fix. If the deal ultimately caves in, the sellers and their agent are going to have to start their marketing process all over again—and who knows how many potential buyers were missed during the interval.

So, going back, at the time the purchase agreement is submitted, the buyers usually haven't given much thought to who should inspect the house—so they turn to their real estate agent and say, "Who do you recommend?"

The Referral

The vast (vast, vast, vast) majority of home inspection jobs come as referrals from real estate agents (as you saw in Chapter 7), and real estate agents have myriad feelings about home inspectors. Agents literally run the gamut from wanting to recommend no one at all to recommending a specific person, hopefully you.

It would be very wise of you, by the way, to make sure you understand whether your state regulates how consumers find you. In very few states, real estate agents are simply instructed to make no recommendations at all regarding home inspectors. In other states, laws require that the consumer be given a list of every home inspector in the state. (From the consumer's point of view, of course, neither of those approaches is especially helpful.)

In states where there are no regulations, real estate agents may be bound by their office policies or, perhaps, their personal policies. But typically, when consumers ask agents which home inspector they recommend, the response is one of the four described below.

1. "Here's the Yellow Pages, find one yourself."

This agent is afraid of recommending anyone, with the key words being *negligent referral.* The agent is so fearful the home inspector will miss something important that could come back to haunt the agent—and by "haunt" we mean "lawsuit." This is not a completely unfounded fear. The agent worries that if he refers the consumer to an inspector and the inspector does a lousy job, not only will the consumer sue the inspector but she also will sue the real estate agent who referred the inspector—a "negligent referral."

So rather than recommend anyone, the agent will simply hand the phone book over to the consumer and say, "Find one yourself."

(It should be noted that the "Find one yourself" option actually is on the wane. Most courts are essentially deciding that if agents do basic due diligence, or have experience working with someone they feel is a quality inspector and with whom they've never had a problem, then why should the agents be hung if the inspector happens to have a bad day and blow the job?)

The next typical response:

2. "Here's a list of inspectors our company has worked with in the past."

For the consumer, this is a little better than "Find one yourself." Here the agent is giving the consumer perhaps 10 or 12 names. But it is still up to the consumer to make the choice and actually hire the inspector. Again note, however, that all the consumer has is names on a sheet of paper. This agent expects the customers to do their own due diligence, check the right resources, and ask the right questions—even while the clock is ticking on the deal.

Next:

3. "Here's a list of three whom I've used before."

For the consumer, this is a better option. At least he or she has reason to believe the agent has worked with each of the three and been satisfied or they wouldn't be referred. Still, however, the investigative work is left to the consumer.

And finally:

4. "I do a lot of work with this home inspector. I recommend him (or her)."

This is what happens in a growing number of transactions. It is still left to the consumer to actually hire the inspector, and certainly the consumer is free to hire someone else, but essentially the agent is saying, "I trust this person—you can, too."

And typically, considering the time and pressure constraints the buyers are under, they usually are going to say something like "Fine by me."

What the consumer normally does not ask the real estate agent, however, is the follow-up question: "What did this home inspector do to earn your endorsement?"

Representing the House

Alan Carson, head of Carson Dunlop in Toronto, who has been around the home inspection business in the United States and Canada since 1978, says he believes home inspectors should take the attitude that regardless of who hires them, they represent the house in the deal.

"**W**here you see the question arise about swaying the report one way or the other is usually with a marginal real estate agent working with a marginal home inspector. They are both trying too hard to get something out of the deal. Neither will last long in the business," says Alan Carson. ∎

As homes age, he reasons, they develop certain problems and peculiarities. All homes do. A house is what it is; it is simply up to the inspector to recognize its curiosities when he or she sees them and report them faithfully.

If a buyer is interested in buying a home that is older, that buyer should not expect it to be in "new home" condition, nor should a seller try to kid anyone that it is. Home inspectors should not be intimidated into swaying their reports to the positive, but neither is there a need to exaggerate the negative.

Carson remembers when putting pressure on home inspectors was virtually a given. In the early days of the industry—in the late 1960s and early 1970s—the need for home inspections was still being established. "There was always pressure to color a report one way or another. The buyer wanted to renegotiate the deal so he'd want a 'hard inspection.' But the listing agent didn't want you to be too hard on the house because he wanted the deal to go through. And he wouldn't use you again if you were too hard and he'd make sure everyone knew it. You were being pulled in every direction."

As the inspection industry has matured and achieved a high degree of acceptance, the pendulum has swung back the other way.

"Good real estate agents are anxious to have an inspection," Carson says. "They want to move the liability onto the inspector in case it turns up later that something is wrong with the house."

And When the Seller Is the Client?

Again, who your client is and whom you represent are sometimes different things. And when the seller is the paying customer, it is even more important for you—the inspector—to represent the house.

Real estate agents on the listing side are putting more pressure on their sellers to have their homes inspected before even putting the house on the market. The logic is that the inspector will be able to identify issues that the seller may not even be aware of and that the seller will have time to fix those problems before the "For Sale" sign goes up in the front yard.

Agents believe a preinspected home, especially if the report is made available to any serious buyer who comes in the front door, is a marketing plus. First, the buyer is made aware of issues with the property. And second, the buyer is on notice that those issues have been accommodated for in the price the seller has set.

There are two problems with that course of action, however. The obvious one is that many buyers, on the advice of their buyer agents, are not going to trust the seller's home inspector to provide an honest view of the home.

The less obvious problem, however, is that most sellers are responding unenthusiastically to the idea of hiring their own inspector and making their homes' faults public.

On the day most sellers decide to put a home on the market, they mentally pack and prepare to move. They see no reason to invest more money in a house they no longer will occupy. Save it for the house they move to.

Also, many sellers feel the inspector is there to make a liar out of them or to tell the world that they have done a lousy job of keeping up the house.

The seller may feel the house is in good repair, and may even make notations to that effect on the seller disclosure form. But the seller's afraid the inspector is going to find out differently.

Plus, many sellers still believe they will be able to "put one over" on both the buyer and the buyer's home inspector. If the buyer's inspector doesn't discover a defect (which quite likely will be known, but undisclosed by the seller), the seller feels he's gotten off free. The defect now becomes the buyer's problem and the seller hasn't had to pay a thing.

Needless to say, in a society where people will go to court at the drop of a hat, that position is becoming ever more risky.

CHAPTER 9

Getting Paid

You can make $100,000 your first year, but you may not pocket enough to live on.

If you're serious about trying the home inspection business, you need to figure out what it's going to take for you to make a living at it.

You have your tools. You have your training. You're ready to go. Someone calls you up to book an inspection, and what's one of the first things they ask?

Your rate.

In the back of your mind you're thinking about all the money you've just spent—to get that training, to obtain a license, to buy liability and/or Errors and Omissions insurance (required by some states and some groups), to purchase your tools, to buy a computer, to start your marketing, and so on and on. Meanwhile, you also have other real-life expenses—paying for your vehicle, gas, health insurance, your own living arrangements, and things like food.

Considering all that, you're thinking a fee in the $10,000 range might be a good place to start.

Of course, that's where your home inspection career would end.

The reality is that nationwide, the average fee for a traditional home inspection falls somewhere between $250 to $500. But the going rate in your area could be lower, or it could be higher.

There is an assortment of other variables you will eventually want to factor in when setting your fee: size of the house, its age, and whether the client wants to add on some inspection-related services you might also be trained to provide, such as extensive inspections for termites or asbestos. Does the house have a pool, and are you expected to inspect that as well? Time is money, and all these affect how much time you'll spend at a house. But for now, we're talking general rates.

Real estate agents, of course, are paid on a commission basis, so what they make depends on the price of the house. Home inspectors, however, typically have been unable to make the argument that they also should be paid according to the price. Consumers tend to argue "A crack in a wall is a crack in a wall, whether it's a $200,000 house or a $2 million house."

Many inspectors who charge by the size of a home will set a minimum fee—maybe in the $150 to $200 price range—then charge 10 to 12 cents per square foot after that. Before telling a consumer how much you charge, however, be sure to ask whether you'll be inspecting a basement, and how many bathrooms the house has, and whether it is one, two, or three stories.

All these things could factor into how long it will take to inspect the house and, as noted, time is money.

In justifying your rate, you may want to mention whether the client will be getting the inspection report immediately, or to what degree you'll be making yourself available for questions from the buyer, the buyer's agent, the seller or even the listing agent. Communication takes time and (how many times do we have to say it?) time is money.

In researching this book, we found an inspector who advertised his prices this way:

- 0–1,000 square feet: $350.00
- 1,000–1,500 sq. ft.: $395.00
- 1,500–2,500 sq. ft.: $425.00

- 2,500–3,500 sq. ft.: $450.00
- More than 3,500 sq. ft.: Call for quote

He charged a little less per square foot for condos and town-houses, and considerably less for mobile homes. The difficulty factor in inspecting commercial properties, he said, was so variable that he could not set a standard fee. He needed to have an extensive description of the property before he could submit a bid.

He also charged a reinspection fee of $125. (A reinspection is when he would inspect a property, write a report, and then be called back for a reinspection to make sure any repairs suggested had been satisfactorily completed.)

Also, many home inspectors these days are charging "cancellation fees" and "missed appointment" fees. Just like doctors and dentists, if the client doesn't show up, not only are you out the time you've waited but also the fee you would have collected.

So, How Much Should You Charge?

"It really depends on what part of the country you're in," notes Mallory Anderson, executive director of the National Association of Home Inspectors. "In California and New York, the average home inspection is $300 to $400. In South Dakota, you're not going to charge somebody that. You have to look at the state's economy and what homes are selling for."

The key words you need to remember are *in your area.*

Like real estate, all home inspection is local.

It doesn't matter what fellow franchisees might charge across the state or around the country, or what inspectors in your state or national organization think is a fair price.

It may not even matter what you think is a fair price.

What really matters first is what most of the others in your inspection area are charging.

Not that you want to charge the same amount. (How does that distinguish you from them?) But you also don't want to be too far off the mark either. That could make prospective clients a little nervous if they've already heard a figure for what most home inspections cost (from the real estate agent, friends, brochures, etc.).

So, it's time to do a little research.

To see what other inspectors in your area charge, take a look at their newspaper and telephone book ads, check Web sites, or even call their offices.

But be careful about discussing fees directly with other inspectors in your area.

"You can set yourself up for litigation and being challenged," says Stan Garnet, an 11-year home inspector with Inspectors Associates based in Atlanta and a member of ASHI's Public Relations Committee.

Accusations of unfair trade practices or price-fixing could put a crimp on your career, to say the least.

"We would love to see it where there is more emphasis on where fees should be," Garnet adds, "and what a home inspector should look to be charging. You can't tell someone how to set their fees.

"We know there are home inspectors out there, at least they call themselves home inspectors, that charge $150 to $200 when we've got an average fee for that house of $300 to $400. The more experienced home inspectors that don't need to lower fees to get business are going to collect $350 to $500 for that inspection."

Don Norman, the managing instructor for Inspection Training Associates in Chicago, believes it costs the average urban inspector at least $125 in overhead to do an inspection. "That's how much it costs me to get in my truck. I see inspectors charging $150 to $200 for an inspection. Those people have no idea what it costs to do business."

Stephen Gladstone of Stamford, Connecticut, a former president of ASHI, suggests that most new people coming into the business have no idea what it costs to run a business, and therefore have little grasp of what to charge.

"A lot of people don't know how to make up a business plan," he says. "They don't know how much it costs to run a vehicle or how much their equipment costs. How much does it cost to have a telephone in the office and someone to answer it? What's the Internet cost? How much does it cost to produce the report?"

Add advertising and other promotion to your overhead costs. "When you're first starting out, you may need to advertise. That's an expense. And clothes so you'll look professional," says Gladstone, who runs a Kaplan Home Inspection Training School.

There also is training, and Errors and Omissions insurance.

Gladstone believes a good business plan can tell an entrepreneur what monthly expenses may be. But that's just enough to keep the doors open. You still have the costs of feeding yourself and your family, supporting your mortgage or rent, and other life expenses.

"All those things have to go into figuring out how much to charge."

Michelle Teague, also an inspector in Chicago, says her fee depends on a variety of factors: square footage of the home, single-family home vs. condo, in an urban area or rural setting, and the age.

"Price is a challenge," she says. An inspection in one part of town could cost $325, but a similar home in another part of the city could cost $400 or more to inspect just because it will present different difficulties. "You can't forget about the time it takes to travel between appointments. Similar houses could be in dramatically different conditions."

Kimberly St. Louis of A-PRO Home Inspection Service in Madison, Wisconsin, says her average fee is $270 based on the age of the home and its square footage, although she charges much less for condos and townhouses.

"I just called and asked around a lot. I got online. Then I priced myself a little bit lower. But I'm also a single person so I can charge a little less," she says.

Alyssa Hickson of National Inspection Corp. in Malabar, Florida, said she and her husband dropped their fees a bit in the beginning but after about 50 inspections, pushed them back up.

"So many people assume that if you cost a little bit more, you're better. Don't undercut. Look at everybody else's rate and then calculate how much training you have and how confident you are, and whether you can successfully market yourself.

"We looked at the ads a local termite pest control company was running that they said were not the cheapest but they were the best. And they have the most business, so we went along with the same thing."

Shelly Barroner and her husband, who launched HomeTeam Inspection Services in central Pennsylvania, said their research revealed three different price structures. They first chose a price between the ranges, but found it difficult to attract the amount of business they were hoping for in their predominantly rural area.

"Then we dropped to the lowest price range. We got a few more but it's still not where we would like it to be."

Troy Bloxom of Home Inspection Plus in Eagle River, Alaska, says he typically charges $325 "unless it's a gargantuan house."

"Part of it is I researched what everyone else was charging. I decided to pick the middle of the road. I decided not to be a cut-rate inspector because people know you typically get what you pay for. I also didn't want to be the highest," says Bloxom.

But the issue of cut-rate fees goes beyond the question of whether it's a smart way to boost business.

Take a very close look at the big picture, warns Dennis R. Robitaille of Saugus, Massachusetts, a licensed home inspector since 1982 and founder of the Independent Home Inspectors of North America.

"A lot of inspectors make the inspection fee a real big issue. They think by offering the cheapest fee out there, that's going to get them the home inspection so they're offering home inspections as low as $195," he explains.

"The average home in Massachusetts has to be going for at least $400,000. For $195, why would home inspectors go out there and make themselves liable for that $400,000 house?"

With all that in mind, let's go back to the original question: What do you say when callers ask for your rate?

Some inspectors contend the best response is not to tell them—yet.

Instead, they recommend you respond by talking about what you have to offer. Tell callers that you are locally owned and operated, what organizations you belong to, and try to answer—without even being asked—any other questions you think callers should be asking you ("We offer a 24-hour turnaround time on reports"; "We go beyond the standards of practice of our state, and of course—clearly explain the limits of a home inspection"; etc.).

They say you should speak relatively slowly so callers can write down your information, in effect creating a sort of sales brochure.

Why do this first? Some callers are just price-shopping, that's true. But often, callers ask about prices because they simply don't know what else to ask.

The price-shoppers want the lowest possible price because they see the home inspection as just another step in the process, rather than a critical link. You need to explain why they don't want the cheapest inspector evaluating a product that is so important and so expensive—their future home.

The National Association of Certified Home Inspectors (NACHI) advises inspectors:

"Emphasize the relative difference between the extra amount you charge above and beyond your competitor and the price of the item (house) you are inspecting. Example: 'Two hundred fifteen thousand, nine hundred dollars is an expensive purchase. Spend the extra $85 and use me. I know I'm a little expensive, but very little compared to the price of the home you're buying.'"

NACHI recommends that inspectors offer to fax prospective clients a price list, but then also to fax a brochure, other promotional material, any reference letters, a copy of the Code of Ethics they follow, and, if a member of NACHI, the membership certificate.

"Prospective clients have almost no way to determine which inspector is the best from brochures. However, they believe that the best costs the most. For example: If you are in an area where your competition is charging $275, raise your prices $55 to $330," says NACHI.

NACHI believes most clients are shopping for the best inspector, not the cheapest.

"Raising your price will get you more inspection work. If a price shopper acts startled by your prices, ask him or her how much the home they're buying costs. Then say, 'Wow, that's a lot of money. A home inspection is no place to skimp. You'd better spend the extra $55 and have *me* inspect it."

And don't forget to talk about the type of report they'll be receiving as part of your fee. If you provide anything in written form beyond your comments as you go through the house—as most clients expect—your report will be a valuable resource for years to come, whether it as simple as a filled-in form, as elaborate as a PowerPoint or video presentation, or somewhere in between.

Getting Paid

The most important question: When do you get paid? The easy answer is, When does your written and signed contract say you should be paid?

The vast majority of home inspectors advise their clients that payment is due on completion of the inspection. Many inspectors, at the time they are hired, will advise the client that they expect to be paid in cash (some inspectors never accept checks), although a growing number of inspectors also now accept credit cards.

Experience has taught them not to release the inspection report until they are paid.

Needless to say, you need to be up front about that during the phone call when you are hired. Be very blunt that you expect payment at the time the service is rendered and what form you want that payment to take—again, usually cash.

There are, however, going to be times when homebuyers, sellers and real estate agents will attempt to negotiate with you on when the fee is paid. They may ask that you wait for your money until the deal closes and the other fees (to the agents, the title companies, the lawyers, etc.) get paid. Some inspectors will accept that delay, but they also will charge extra for the wait. We have seen inspectors tack on an extra $50 to $75 if they have to wait for the close to get their money.

As always, the important thing is to make sure your clients understand up front what your billing policy is. You owe it to your client—and yourself—to make sure there are no surprises when it comes to getting paid.

CHAPTER 10

How Busy Can You Be? It Depends.

The realities of endless possibilities . . .

Now that you're imagining huge dollar signs on the front door of every house that needs to be inspected, you also may believe that you will have no trouble making $1,000 or more every day you want to work (just like the ads promise).

Don't be going to the bank just yet.

You need to understand the realities, even under the best-case scenario.

Assume for the moment that you are receiving more calls for inspections than you can possibly handle (see Chapter 6 for ways to make that happen). Let's pretend that every single day, seven days a week, many people want you to inspect houses. The possibilities and potential to fatten your bank account seem endless.

But there are some important obstacles on your road to success. Even when all of your dreams of too much business come true, there are just going to be some things that you can't control. And those things will put major restraints on just how busy you can be in a day or a week or a month.

Briefly:

First, there's geography.

You may have noticed that every house that needs inspection isn't on the same street or in the same neighborhood or even in the same town. It will take you time—sometimes lots of time—to travel from your base of operations to the house to be inspected and then on to your next appointment. It could be across town, in the next community, in the next county, or even in the next state.

Second, there's the time required to do the inspection.

The fact is that if you want repeat business through the same buyer, seller, or real estate agent, you have to do a really good job. That means taking the time to inspect everything that needs to be inspected—no shortcuts. And then at the end, depending on how you operate, at the very least you most likely will be explaining your findings to your client either briefly or in depth.

Let's not forget that in between the time you arrive and the time you depart, the client is likely to be accompanying you on your inspection. That's just one of the things the client is paying for: a personal, expert tour of the house (for more on this, see Chapter 13).

But that also will slow you down when the client, particularly a first-time buyer, asks question after question while you are trying to concentrate on the task at hand.

Then there's the issue of blocked access to the places you are supposed to inspect. It could take you time to move things, to set up ladders and take them down, or to wait for someone to find the key to open that basement door.

Third, there's the report time.

Again, depending on how you operate, it takes time to write up your report. You may have fancy electronic equipment to speed the process, or you may not. Some inspectors like to provide a brief overview on site and then go back to the office to put together the in-depth version. It could include photographs or videotape or other items that take some time to pull together.

Fourth, there's your physical limits.

Can you do that third inspection of the day with as much enthusiasm and care as the first, crawling over things and climbing ladders, or will you just plain be too tired? Do you need to eat sometime during the day or sleep more than a few hours a night? Do you want to take a day or two off during the week like most folks?

The Real-Life Variables

We've just talked about some of the general factors that affect how busy you can be. Now it's time to consider the additional variables that can either hinder, or help, opportunities to maximize your time and, therefore, your earning potential.

Yes, we know. Every house is unique. But really, most houses are physically constructed the same way. The biggest variables involve style—one floor or two or more, finished basements or no basement at all, attic or crawlspace, and so forth.

As an inspector, you will find these style variables will have huge impacts on your time and energy. Styles can vary by neighborhood, by town, by state, and by region.

"An inspection averages two and a half to three hours, but there are exceptions. I don't think anyone can do more than three a day in this area," says John Merritt of Santa Rosa, California. "But it's different in other areas of southern California where you have primarily slab construction (no basement to inspect) or tile roofs so you can't walk on the roofs."

Another major variable is the square footage of the home you're inspecting, says Mallory Anderson of the National Association of Home Inspectors.

"We highly recommend that inspectors not do more than three a day, and in the busy season, that could be about 15 a week. If you do a mini-home inspection, those don't take as long. If you do two and a half hours per inspection, you can do three."

Likewise, it depends on the size of the house. Condos take less time. Most homes range in size from 1,500 to 2,200 square feet. But if it's a bigger house—4,000 to 5,000 square feet—you could be there all day.

Which is why charging by the square foot is the preferred option of many inspectors (see previous chapter).

Michael Casey, an 18-year home inspector who also helps run 11 inspection schools across the country, says "for most of the customers, you can do two or three" inspections per day. Many inspectors do fill in some type of form, which adds about a half hour of time to filling out a report. Others spend an hour or longer.

"Quite a few inspectors do 10 to 15 a week. That's about the average. I don't like to do any more than two (per day)—the third one gets to be kind of a grind. I'm not as young as I used to be and it makes for a long day."

One major reality you need to remember when trying to predict your earnings potential is that in nearly every case, you are part of a real estate transaction. And as in real estate, home inspection is not a five-day-a-week, 9-to-5 job. When someone wants to close a real estate deal, you do not have the luxury of extra time to schedule an appointment too far ahead. In most cases, the buyers have mentally purchased the house and you are likely to be a key factor in whether they also physically sign the contract to buy that house. They want answers, and what they really wanted was to have your report yesterday—not in a few days, or a few weeks.

So when someone calls to schedule an inspection, they don't want to wait until it's convenient for you. If you don't fit into their timetable, they will hire someone else who will.

You want to be accommodating to get the business. But you also need to be able to do more than one inspection a day. That means there will be times when you will have to stretch the limits of your workday by beginning earlier in the morning and ending later in the evening.

There is also the reality of the local real estate market. In a buyer's market, real estate moves at a slower pace while buyers choose among the many homes available. In a seller's market, with limited inventory, real estate offers and counteroffers can move at a frenzied pace.

"If I am in a heavy seller's market, I literally get 24 hours' notice or they'll go somewhere else," says Frank Poliferno of AmeriSpec in West Nyack, New York. "If you look at my calendar three days out, there's nothing on it."

> **"A** lot of how busy you can be depends on what your willingness is to work," says Lynette Gebben of AmeriSpec in Madison, Wis. "You can work as early as 8:30 in the morning or earlier, up to say 9:30 at night." ∎

Working at the whim of the real estate market can be unnerving if you have a compulsion to plan ahead. Also unnerving is the reality that because you are part of the real estate transaction, there are other parts of that deal that could fall through. When that happens, like dominoes falling, your scheduled inspection also falls through, despite the fact that you may have turned away other business for that time slot.

"If you have a good property, it can have multiple bids," says Poliferno. "The inspection can get canceled because they lost the bid. It's very frustrating. I lost two yesterday, and to lose $1,000 like that is very tough."

Markets go up and down. But one thing doesn't change. Any inspector needs to complete a certain number of inspections every year just to stay afloat.

"You need at least 250 a year to stay in business," says Ralph Wirth, former NAHI president and a 20-year inspector in Louisville, Kentucky. "We used to call them the $60,000 men. If you don't generate over $60,000 a year, it's very difficult to stay within the industry.

"If you're not above that level, you're not going to be making it."

CHAPTER 11

How Far Does the Inspection Have to Go?

Are you going to be able to restrict your inspection to just the home, or will it go into the yard and down the street?

Hopefully by now you realize the importance of clearly communicating to your client just what a home inspection is—and isn't.

And hopefully by now, you have convinced your client that you do not have X-ray vision, that you do not have the power to see into the future, and that you cannot possibly be an expert on every single system and aspect of the home.

Even if that's what your client expects.

You remind them that first, and foremost, a home inspection is simply an objective visual examination of the readily accessible physical structure and systems of a home—from top to bottom (or roof to foundation).

You also tell your clients it is not an appraisal to set market value, nor is it a municipal inspection to verify that the structure meets codes and local standards. And, unless you are an engineer, it is not an engineering report.

But what does all this really mean in terms of how far you need to go to provide a competent, professional home inspection?

> "I think the biggest thing they don't understand is what we're trying to accomplish. I often use the phrase: 'Inspect, detect, and then direct,'" says Bill Mason of Second Opinion Home Inspection of Sarasota, Florida. ∎

In a very real way, that depends on you.

- It depends on what state you're operating in because that state may dictate the minimum scope of your inspection. Some do, some don't. At this writing, several states don't even license home inspectors, never mind telling them what they should do.

- It depends on what professional organization you belong to because in calling yourself a member of that group, you agree to follow their "standards of practice" detailing the minimum you have to do to call it an inspection. (These could be the same if your state has incorporated a national group's standards as its own.)

- It depends on whether you belong to a franchise that also dictates the minimum level of services you must perform.

- And it depends on how far you believe you should go beyond any standards you are supposed to follow. Do you believe that what you might find beyond the minimum inspection area could affect what happens to the house? And do you remember telling your client that you go beyond the standards of practice?

Although some home inspectors believe that they are only required to take a look at the actual house or maybe an outbuilding or two, the standards of practice of the three largest home inspection groups also require an examination of drainage, grading, and vegetation if they are likely to "adversely affect" the structure.

"Everything is tied in," says Mason. "When you see a doctor, he may hold your wrist, look in your eyes; he's looking for telltale signs while he's talking to you. You've got to look at the whole picture. When you drive up, you notice the grading, you look at the property. "

In addition, says Mason, a home inspector has to be cognizant of where a house sits in relation to other homes and its relative location on a street. For example, if the house is at the end of a street and at the bottom of a hill, the inspector might investigate how—and if—rainwater is diverted from the property.

Nick Gromicko, executive director of the National Association of Certified Home Inspectors, agrees that inspectors ought to be aware of factors outside the four walls of a house that could affect that structure.

"For instance, drainage. That might not only encompass the property line but also past the property line. If water is coming into the basement, the reason might be far from the home," says Gromicko.

But what about all of those other factors that people are concerned about these days? Things like asbestos, geological issues, indoor air quality, manufacturer recalls, and environmental hazards including hazardous waste?

They may be in the standards of practice, too, but listed under the things that inspectors are "not required" to include in their inspections.

So it will be up to you to decide how far you should go. Some of that will be determined by what your competitors are offering. And some of it will be affected by what clients want as the professionalism of the industry continues to grow.

One area that you should consider is keeping up-to-date on product recalls, and relaying that information as a courtesy to your clients. Being a member of a home inspector organization can help you do that because either the group, or fellow members, are likely to pass the information along. In addition, the Consumer Product Safety Commission (*http://www.cpsc.gov/*) has a service that allows you to sign up for free e-mail updates regarding product recalls.

"The average loss from a kitchen fire is $35,000. This can come simply from having an old GE dishwasher that's been recalled and people don't know it. This is where it comes in handy to be part of an organization," says Mason.

Mason says one of his goals is that the insurance industry should require every house that sells to be inspected, adding "there is a need for that information to be provided to the insurance industry to determine the insurability of the house."

Staying Out of Court

The reason for all of these questions, of course, is that everyone is trying to stay out of court, and the question of "How much are buyers entitled to know in advance?" is being asked more and more frequently.

It's easy enough for you, the inspector, to say, "Off-site environmental problems aren't part of the inspection," but that won't necessarily keep you from being sued. (Although if you say it in a written, signed contract, that could help you enormously.)

You may think you are simply being asked to look around a property, but is it possible that someday you'll be asked to look up as well? In St. Louis not long ago homeowners complained they should have been warned about airport noise because they weren't aware a new runway would bring flights directly overhead. Whose responsibility is it to know that?

In New Jersey just a few years ago a group of buyers of new homes ended up suing their developer and real estate agents because they failed to disclose there was a landfill dump within a half-mile of the development. Chemicals from the landfill eventually began leaching across the new home properties. The owners were outraged.

The developer and real estate agents said they shouldn't have to disclose things that are outside the borders of the property. First, they argued, how could anyone really know what things exist outside the property tract and, second, they noted that at the time the homes were built the seepage wasn't a problem.

The trial court disagreed, saying the property owners should have been told of the proximity of the landfill.

Are these the kind of things inspectors will have to know in the future? Possibly. More real estate agents are urging buyers to hire home inspectors. One of the reasons is that agents want to put inspectors on the hook for problems and take themselves off.

As real estate agents continue to strive to simply be agents of the transfer of the property, you definitely can expect them to try to shuffle more disclosure issues onto inspectors.

CHAPTER 12

How Dangerous Is This Job?

Imagine what you'd look like standing naked on someone's roof.

"Is the home inspection business dangerous?" you ask. In the spirit of the infamous slogan, "Guns don't kill people, people kill people," we can unequivocally answer, "No. The home inspection business isn't dangerous—just the people who are in it."

In the course of our research we talked to a wide number of very experienced home inspectors who will assure you this is not a dangerous profession. Yet every one of them seems to have a harrowing story of a narrow escape. But all those stories seem to start with the words, "I knew I shouldn't have put the ladder there . . ." or "I knew I was standing in water when . . ." or "I always shine the flashlight in the crawlspace first, but this one time . . ."

As you've already read, and will continue to read, the home inspection business is a visual business. You are not obligated to crawl on a roof if you can see it from the top of the ladder, or even better, through binoculars from the ground.

You are not obligated to stick a screwdriver into a crack in the foundation; if you don't know what that dark thing in the crawl-space is, you are not obligated to poke it with your flashlight; and if you see a bee in the attic and think you hear other bees in the attic, you might want to assume it's a nest.

Most of all, you have not been hired to do heroic deeds for a few hundred dollars. You don't have to read the rest of this chapter if you'll just remember these words: "If it looks life-threatening, don't do it."

A Few True Stories

The first rule of home inspecting is that it is easier to get on a roof than it is to get off. This story comes from an inspector who knows that firsthand.

According to him, it had rained all morning, but the sun came out in the afternoon and it was going to be a nice day. As this particular inspector made his inspection of the outside of the house, he was aware the grass was wet but didn't think too much about it.

Finally, he retrieved his ladder from the truck and put it up against the back of the house—not paying much attention to where he placed it. He went up without a problem, feeling the ladder sink in just a bit as he ascended.

It wasn't until he was finished surveying the roof that he realized he had a problem.

When he crossed his leg over to put his foot on the top rung, he could feel the ladder slide out from the bottom. He pulled the ladder up a bit from the top and tried to replace it firmly on the ground, but when he crossed over again, again he could feel it slide.

Once again he pulled up the ladder from the top and this time repositioned it a few feet to the left, then a few feet to the right. Each time he tried to get on it he could feel it give way from the bottom.

"I felt as stupid as I could possibly feel," he confessed.

The homebuyer hadn't accompanied him on the inspection, and the listing agent had left some time before. The seller wasn't at home.

"I knew I could go ahead and get on the ladder, but if it slid out from under me, I was going to go crashing down, and since I was at the back of the house, I wasn't even sure anyone would notice me."

Homes in the area were relatively far apart, but the inspector nevertheless shouted "HELP!" a few times, to no avail. He crawled over to the front of the roof and attempted to wave down cars as they went by. The drivers either didn't see him or just waved back.

"The only thing I could think to do was take off all my clothes and stand there on the roof waving. I figured someone eventually would notice a naked crazy man standing on a roof and call the police."

Fortunately, just before he started stripping, the homeowner came home.

The inspector was rescued with body and dignity intact.

Another inspector willingly concedes, "For the most part, home inspecting is not a dangerous business, even though there probably is some risk in every inspection. Usually if there is an injury, it is because of carelessness or sheer stupidity by the inspector."

While saying he had never actually been hurt in an inspection, he knew of peers who had—mostly broken bones from falling off roofs or the occasional electrical shock. (Ladders and power lines do not mix. The rule is: Look twice, climb once.)

This veteran did have a few ladder stories, however.

"I put the ladder flat on a lower roof without tying it down. While I was standing on it, the ladder slipped. It fell to the ground and I ended up hanging off a gutter. Fortunately there was a construction worker there who helped me get off the roof. There was a lot of damage to the gutter."

Another time during an inspection in a low-income part of an urban area, there was another ladder problem.

"It was a flat roof, but the ladder shifted while I was climbing up. The tenant in the building was there and I asked him to reset the ladder. But he couldn't speak English and we were having a hard time communicating. Pretty soon I hear a scraping. I hear him moving the ladder. I yell at him to stop and he drops it against the electrical service wire to the house. Not a good situation.

"I'm motioning him to stay away from the ladder. Don't touch the ladder. In the meantime, I'm wondering how I'm going to get off the roof.

"He runs around the side of the house. In the garage there is another ladder and he brings it around. But it's about five feet too short and almost vertical to the ground. He wants me to hang off the edge and lower myself down until my feet touch the ladder. I figure I'm more likely to fall to my death."

In the end: "He called the fire department and they took me off with a hook and ladder truck. The lesson I learned was to always tie off the ladder."

Crawlspaces also are a favorite spot of home inspectors and other critters.

"I have a 25,000-candlepower flashlight," said another inspector. "Before I ever go into a crawlspace, I take that thing and shine it around in there. That thing throws a lot of light and you want that for crawlspaces and attics because you never know what you're going to find."

A lapse in that routine, however, brought a scary experience.

"I don't know why, but this one time I pushed my head and shoulders in about halfway before I turned on the light. I was face to face with a big old possum and he was just smiling at me and showing his teeth. I just smiled right back and backed out of there as fast as I could."

Crawlspaces also, of course, are favorite habitats of bees, bats, rodents of all variety, and the occasional rattlesnake. They can be even more uncomfortable, however, when accompanied by standing water and dangling wires. "With everything else you're doing trying to move your body, you accidentally touch something and that's it, you get shocked," an inspector said. "Hopefully, you live to tell about it."

One trainer who teaches new people coming into the industry says he emphasizes, "You're not being paid enough to put your life in danger, so don't do it. If whoever has hired you asks you to do something you're not comfortable with, say so. Walk away if you have to."

The trainer also said inspectors need to be especially careful when a homebuyer is in tow.

"They put their hands where they shouldn't and they get shocked or burned," he said. "I know of buyers who followed their inspector into the attic. One buyer stepped down but missed the framing and fell through. You do need to protect your buyers."

And most of all, he said, "When you're doing an inspection, make sure you know who else is in the house. You do not want young kids following you around. You don't want young kids playing Junior Home Inspector and plugging things into electrical panels."

Sometimes What You Don't See Can Be Problematic Too

Another curious thing you'll find is that when you are in the house, everybody else is going to assume you're in charge.

That means if you open a door and the dog runs out, the owner is going to assume you're responsible. (Before you arrive at the property, you need to make sure pets are either tied up or off the premises before you enter.)

Also, you need to be careful to knock on closed doors. You don't want to walk in on the owner while he or she is otherwise involved. And while we're talking about careless owners, make sure you advise homeowners to pick up any valuables they might have laying around. The last thing you need is for a homeowner to report a missing bracelet after you've left.

Yes, these things happen.

So needless to say, not all dangers are associated with the structure of the home. Trainers also warn that if you arrive at a home inspection and for some reason are worried about the neighborhood or the security of your tools and yourself, then you need to be honest with your client. If you have a partner or an apprentice, it's wise to have them hover while you do your work. Otherwise, leave.

Again, balance what you can make from an inspection with what you can lose.

CHAPTER 13

Working with Buyers

Patience is the queen of all virtues–and nowhere is that truer than in the home inspection business.

In a perfect world, you would be able to thoroughly preplan your home inspection and carry it out with military precision. You would be efficient. You would be undistracted by anyone or anything. You would be able to study the various components of a home, and then step back and take in the whole Zen experience of the house without outside interference.

Well, that's not going to happen, so forget it.

The truth is, you often are going to have the homebuyer in tow; sometimes a disgruntled seller will be hovering over your shoulder; occasionally the buyer's real estate agent will be hanging around and, who knows, maybe even the listing agent.

You can always try to ignore everyone else and concentrate just on the house. Or you can accept the reality that dealing with other people is part of the job, and trying to accommodate them is the path of least resistance. Yes, of course, your pleasant demeanor could mean repeat business and referrals (and maybe fewer lawsuits). But more importantly, the whole process is going to go better if you're tactful and friendly to everyone who encroaches on your airspace.

(As a practical matter, veteran real estate agents don't really want to be at the inspection and consider it a hand-holding exercise that wastes their time. If listing agents show up at all, you can expect them to remember they have to make an important phone call and they'll catch up to you later. The buyer's agent will probably offer to go help the listing agent dial his or her cell phone. The homeseller will probably give up a few minutes later, convinced you're an incompetent charlatan whose sole purpose is to drive down a fair, honest, and thoroughly justified price. Oh well.)

Even so, you may need to keep repeating to yourself that you're a professional, and you have no vested interest in how the deal ultimately turns out. A callous way of looking at it is that you get paid one way or the other. A somewhat gentler way is to simply acknowledge that it takes a lot of components to make a house—and one of the most important is the human component.

Your Bedside Manner

For you, the home inspection process begins during the phone call when you're hired. You are collecting a number of pieces of data from the client: location of the home, when the inspection has to be done, possibly the age of the home, number of rooms, and square footage. You're going to want a callback number for the client (and a couple of alternatives), a fax number, and maybe an e-mail address.

Buyers also are going to want to know certain things from you. Your price, of course. Hopefully, they'll be asking for your credentials and referrals, how long you have been in business, and whether you have any designations. These are all good questions that demonstrate that the buyers have done a little research into the importance of the home inspection and take it seriously.

Even if the buyers don't ask those questions, as we've mentioned before, you should find some way to work them into the conversation.

But you and the client also are going to want to exchange views on a number of other things.

You'll almost certainly be asked how long the inspection will take—and you'll have to explain that all you can give is a ballpark figure. The client will probably want to know when your report will be ready—and you'll explain your company procedures.

In some soft (but assertive) way, you will want to stress the appointment time. You may want to say things like, "If you're delayed, will there be someone there to let me into the house?" Or, "If you're running behind, should I go ahead and start inspecting the outside without you?"

Time is money.

You will want to know whether the client will be joining you on the home inspection or sending a representative (his real estate agent, her father-in-law). One of the things you can count on is that if a homebuyer joins you—especially a first-time homebuyer— the length of the inspection will probably increase to accommodate questions. *But make no mistake: You* do *want the buyer to come along. In the end, it is easier for questions to be asked and answered on the spot, rather than through a series of phone calls after your report has been sent over.*

But also keep in mind that there is a difference between having buyers "observe" the inspection and "participate" in the inspection. If buyers insist on participating, consider recommending that they bring their own moderately powered flashlight and a small notebook and pen to make their own notes. Needless to say, suggest they wear clothes they can get dirty in.

Under no circumstances should they bring screwdrivers or pliers. Emphasize, politely, that they won't be touching anything.

In that phone conversation, you might also ask if the clients have any special concerns about the house or "Is there anything especially important to you that you might have seen at the house that you'd like me to be sure to check out?" You'll be surprised at the number of times they do have questions, such as mentioning a crack behind a dresser or a ceiling that appears to have been freshly painted.

IT IS CRITICALLY IMPORTANT in this first phone call that you explain the parameters of the inspection. You need to explain what your work will cover, and what it won't. You need to explain what state law, your organization, or local custom obligate you to do, and what you cannot and will not do. You need to be as precise as possible in discussing what you will do for the fee that you'll earn. You also need to discuss what additional fees may be involved if they would like you to provide additional services (such as radon testing, etc.).

You need to advise them that everything you have discussed will be reduced to writing in a contract that eventually will have both parties' signatures at the bottom. (It is incredibly important for both of you that your contract be written and signed. If something goes wrong in the deal, you—or they—will want to be able to go back to your original agreement to see how the issue is addressed. And, in a worst-case scenario, your written contract could become your most important evidence in a lawsuit.)

On Location

When you get to the site of the inspection, you are going to want to repeat much of the conversation you had on the phone. You are going to need to remind them again of what you will and won't do, what your fee covers, and what the procedures are for requesting more tests. Now is the time to get their signatures on the contract.

Much of this, of course, is just practical, common sense advice. But you'd be surprised at the number of misunderstandings that can arise, and the number of lawsuits that can be generated by the words: "I didn't know that he (or she) didn't inspect . . ."

Also, once you are on location (and you can carve this in stone), you may believe your job is just to report on the condition of the property—and every state law and home inspector organization in the land will back you up on that 100 percent—but the homebuyer (especially the first-time homebuyer) will have a different agenda. In addition to wanting you to find everything that's "wrong" with the house, he or she also is hoping you will explain how the house actually works.

The buyers will want you to be their guide to home construction and even do-it-yourself projects. You are probably going to end up pointing out every water shutoff valve in the house, and maybe showing where to kill the electricity in an emergency. If you're lucky, the circuit-breaker box will be neatly (and accurately) labeled. If not, you may end up spending some extra time there, trying to figure it out and explaining, "This switch turns off the power to the kitchen . . . That switch kills the power to the children's bedrooms . . ."

What you are specifically being paid for is to assess the condition of the house. But what the homebuyer is paying for is that you'll also be able to answer questions like these:

- "Why is this pipe here?" and "Why is it hot?"
- "Should that wire be hanging down?" and "Where does it go?"
- "I want to turn these two rooms into one master bedroom. Can I take out this wall?"
- "Do you think I can do this (repair, modification, installation, etc.) myself, or should I call a professional?"
- And invariably, "How much do you think it would cost to do that?"

It's important to remember that your inspection is the first time the homebuyer has actually had a chance to thoroughly go through the inner workings of the house he's already promised to buy. Contractually, how helpful you want to be is up to you. In reality, you are going to find yourself trying to be as helpful as possible.

On the other hand, tread softly. Some of the most innocuous questions can move you into gray areas of ethics. For example:

- "Well, can you fix it?"
- "Do you know somebody who can replace that thing?"

(We get into ethical issues in Chapter 16.)

In the course of the inspection, it is important to remember who you are—but it's also important to remember who you're not. You are a critical observer, not a critic.

It is not up to you to comment on how the house is decorated, or laugh with the buyer when he or she points out the seller's choice of paint color. While clutter could certainly hamper your ability to move around in tight spaces, it is not up to you to declare the current owner a pack rat or a lousy housekeeper.

In some cases, silence is not only golden, it also is professional. However, if you identify the current owner's do-it-yourself project and find it lacking, you do need to express that concern, again as professionally as possible. It may be enough to say that the job appears amateurish or that the owner did not use standard construction practices. Obviously, if a wiring job is so bad that it is unsafe, you need to note that both to the buyer and the seller (or at least the seller's listing agent).

Also, be careful about using words like "not up to code" unless you're sure you know what the code is. Don't try to sound like an expert in something you're not.

It is not up to you to declare "This guy shouldn't have tried to do this himself" or "This guy didn't know what he was doing."

It is your job only to cite the problem with whatever degree of seriousness it may entail. The point is: *Judge the house, not the people.*

That's also true of your own client. If a woman announces she intends to rewire the kitchen herself, it's not up you to suggest she shouldn't do it. It may be appropriate, however, for you to recommend to any buyer that it might be a better idea to have a licensed professional do that kind of work.

Care and Feeding of Clients

Finally, if the homebuyer elects to follow you around the house throughout the inspection, remember that you take on a little bit of responsibility for that buyer's safety, as well as the home's safety.

Needless to say, you should discourage the buyer from crawling up on the roof with you. You may also want to be leery of even bringing a buyer into the attic with you. Buyers have been known to fall through ceilings. (Imagine the seller's surprise, to say nothing of the insurance hassle.)

Obviously, it's better to point out problems in electrical boxes from afar.

And the Report

In the end, of course, everything you've seen in the house is reduced to black ink on white paper and handed to the client. Keep in mind that no matter what casual conversations you've had with the buyer during the course of the inspection or what kind of informal judgments you've made along the way, what really counts is what you put on paper.

When it comes to reopening negotiations on a purchase price, it's one thing for the buyer to claim, "Well, during the inspection the inspector said . . ." and another to say, "Here is what the inspector wrote down in his report."

According to real estate agents, this is where many home inspectors go astray.

Says Bill French of Wm. French Realty in St. Louis, "I want the inspector to give my client his best independent judgment of the home's condition.

"But what I don't want is for him to verbalize to the buyer, 'Well, the roof is shot and needs to be replaced,' but then write in his report, 'The roof is nearing the end of its serviceable life.'

"If the roof is shot, that's a legitimate negotiating point with the seller to get it replaced. But if the roof is going through its cycle of normal wear and tear, then that may not be a negotiating point."

Alternatively, you also want to be careful about being extreme and/or making dramatic statements in showing off your abilities in front of a client. If the furnace isn't firing correctly, say so. But don't say the house could explode at any second. There is nothing more important than accuracy and balance.

Says home inspector Alyssa Hickson of Malabar, Florida, "With most real estate agents, it is the home inspector's demeanor that causes the problem. You don't want to scare people. We are not alarmists. We tell people very matter-of-factly or impress upon them how many things are good."

Getting Along Without You

Should you defend against the do-it-yourselfer?

Very briefly: With the number of home inspections going up every year, and the price of an inspection also moving up, it was foreseeable that a "do-it-yourself" subculture would develop to suggest consumers could inspect their own homes and avoid . . . well . . . you.

There are probably a couple of dozen books out now that take the average homebuyer through the home inspection process, explaining what to look for on the roof, where the problems might be in the basement, how to look at the hot water heater, how to check out the appliances, and so on. There also is an assortment of television shows—usually on the cable channels—that pride themselves on showing the average person how to fix this or that without paying a professional. A lot of them offer videos.

At first blush, it might appear that these things are bad for your business. Clearly, the books and videos are trying to show consumers how to circumvent you. On the other hand, most home inspection professionals aren't worried. In fact, some are even happy to see them. Here's why:

1. Anything that raises consumer consciousness about the need to have a home inspection benefits the industry at large. Simply put: The more people who talk about home inspections, the more people are likely to get home inspections.

2. The reality is that the vast majority of people who buy books about home inspections will not get past the first few pages. Some people simply aren't meant to do the physical work involved in an inspection and they'll end up hiring someone. But they will keep the book as a reference after they've moved in.

3. Most people think they have—but really don't have—the confidence to know for sure that they've done a good job. As soon as they are finished, they start second-guessing themselves, wondering if they forgot something, wondering if "that thing" they saw really was what they thought it was.

4. If it takes a professional, with years of experience and thousands of home inspections under his belt, two to three hours to inspect a home, how long would it take amateurs being guided by a book? A day? Two days? They end up rushing their own job. And don't forget, if it's the buyer doing the inspection—"by the book"—the seller is only giving him or her a limited time in which to get it accomplished. No seller is going to stand around all day waiting for the buyer to figure out what she or he's doing.

5. Liability. When consumers hire a professional home inspector, they are able to shift liability onto that inspector. Alternatively, if they do it themselves and blow their own inspection, they have recourse against no one. And the courts are agreeing. More and more often, judges and juries are ruling that when consumers are given an opportunity to have a professional inspection—and turn it down—they often have no one to blame but themselves for problems that show up later. (There still may be recourse against a seller who has intentionally concealed a defect, but still, juries are more sympathetic when a homebuyer's

claim is backed up with a professional's report.) When a professional home inspector misses something, the opportunity for compensation is much higher.

6. A homebuyer who reads up on how to identify problems in a house may be helping herself weed out homes in the search stage, but also may realize she isn't competent enough to handle the Real Thing when it comes time to buy. Hopefully the book has made her smart enough to "know what she doesn't know," and find someone who does.

7. Hardware. As we cover in Chapter 5, to do a modestly good inspection with any kind of efficiency, it takes an awful lot of specialized tools. Not too many people have those sitting around the house.

8. The other side. How comfortable is any homeseller going to be allowing an unlicensed, unbonded amateur inside his house, poking and probing walls, switching things on and off, and pushing the thermostat way up (and forgetting to turn it back down)? If the do-it-yourself potential buyer damages something, who pays?

9. The do-it-yourselfer is not objective. The do-it-yourselfer is likely to look hard for what he knows about and what concerns him most, at the risk of overlooking other things that could even be more important.

10. For most people, doing your own home inspection simply doesn't make sense. Why would someone spend $400,000 on a home but scrimp on a $400 inspection? Why run the risk of saving $300 on a home inspection but miss a $30,000 foundation problem, or even a $3,000 termite repair?

In fact, most of the do-it-yourself inspection books carry disclaimers that warn consumers not to get in over their heads, and to call a reputable professional if they need to.

So These Books Are No Good?

Here's the irony. No, many of them are very good—so good, in fact, that you may want to consider buying them for your own library.

Many of the do-it-yourself books have actually been written by highly qualified home inspectors with the intent of helping the homebuyer build confidence in his or her purchase. Many provide excellent charts and checklists, photographs of potential problems, and ideas on how they should be handled.

In the right hands, like a professional or someone on their way to becoming a professional, many of these books are excellent references. In the wrong hands, like a homeowner trying to cut corners, they become the old cliché: A little knowledge is a dangerous thing.

So Should Consumers Do Their Own Inspections?

Alan Mooney of Portland, Maine, who founded the national franchise firm Criterium Engineers in the early 1970s, provides at least three reasons why consumers really should hire a professional.

"First of all, the average homebuyers or sellers simply don't have the body of experience necessary to inspect either their own home or a home they want to buy. It's simply too personal. In fact, forget whether or not they have the skills, and forget whether or not they have any of the right experience. The problem is they can't be objective."

Mooney points out that by the time the inspection takes place, "they're already hooked on the house. It's virtually impossible for the average homeowner to be objective at that point in the process."

Second, he says, "there is a difference between reading a book and then going off to do an inspection. The differences in home construction are dramatic from one part of the country to another, from one builder to another, and from one time period to another.

"You wouldn't expect to see the same kind of construction used in a house 50 years old that you'd see in a house that's 10 years old. The new construction isn't necessarily better and the old construction isn't necessarily worse. They're just representative of different periods. Experienced inspectors understand those differences. A book could cover them, but it would have to be pretty big."

Another issue is that when a problem is identified, the novice isn't going to understand whether the problem is large or small. And that could be important.

"You may see a horizontal crack running along the foundation. An experienced inspector is going to know whether the wall needs to be braced, or replaced," Mooney said. "A book isn't going to give you that."

But one of the biggest reasons consumers need professionals is backup.

"Imagine the layman going up against the professional contractor. The layman says, 'This needs to be fixed,' and the contractor comes back and says, 'No it doesn't.' And the layman says, 'Yes it does, it says so in the book.' And the contractor who has been in business for years says, 'The book is wrong.'

"Who is going to back up the consumer in that conflict? Who are you going to believe?"

The professional inspector, reminds Mooney, is there to make sure the consumer can go toe-to-toe in any kind of dispute like that. "When you get a professional inspection, you get representation," he said.

Mooney even goes so far as to suggest that real estate agents buying their own homes, construction workers buying their own homes, and even home inspectors buying their own homes should use professionals.

"A real estate agent may have sold hundreds of homes, and even be familiar with basic construction, but that's not the same as being able to identify problems and know what to do about them. And people in the construction trades need to remember there are 14 different systems in a home. You may know about electrical or plumbing, but that doesn't qualify you to inspect roofs and foundations. And just because you do it one way and the builder of this house did it another way doesn't mean this builder did it wrong."

And even other professional inspectors?

"I've personally done probably close to 20,000 inspections in my life, but I'd still hire an inspector to look at a property I was buying," Mooney said. "You can't be objective when it's your own home."

CHAPTER 15

Liability and the Courts

Lawyers did not create the home inspection business, but they were there at the birth.

There are those who say that today's billion-dollar home inspection industry owes its origins to a California Supreme Court decision handed down in 1984 that had nothing to do with home inspectors and little to do with home defects. The people who say that are not entirely right—but they're not entirely wrong either.

What *Easton v. Strassburger* (152 Cal.App.3d90, 1984) did was strike fear into the hearts of real estate brokers everywhere, and— like releasing the spring-loaded shooter on a pinball machine—it set into motion an issue that is still careening around the home sales industry today.

Look at it this way: In the pinball game of life, the rapid growth of the modern home inspection industry came about because the ball bounced off the brokerage-liability bumper.

Or if you'd like, you can look at it this way: Two-thirds of all litigation between homebuyers and homesellers involves property defects that weren't discovered until after the home was purchased. The vast majority of lawsuits also name the real estate agents involved, and they want to be able to pin the blame on someone else.

Where Did You Come From?

A little history.

If *Easton* represented the blossoming of the home inspection business, then certainly the seeds of that bloom had been planted some 20 years earlier in the consumer activist movements of the 1960s and 1970s—the same movements that brought seat belts to cars, warning labels to cigarettes, and nutrition labels to processed foods.

Consumers were becoming distrustful of Big Business—distrustful that monolithic corporations actually had the best interest of their consumers at heart, and distrustful even that manufacturers would keep unsafe products off the market. It was the dawn of "product liability." Consumers were beginning to try to rebalance the playing field.

According to legal scholars, as early as the mid-1960s the legal premise of "caveat emptor" (let the buyer beware) was being challenged by a new legal notion, "the consumer's right to know." That is, the consumers' right to know what they were getting into before they actually bought something.

In real estate, the 1963 case of *Lingsch v. Savage* (213 Cal.App.2d 729, 735, 1963) established the legal precedent that home listing agents were required to tell buyers about any defects known to them. (Keep in mind that in 1963, the idea that a real estate agent could represent the interest of a buyer was completely foreign. At the time, all agents in the transaction represented the seller's interest because that's who paid them. The listing agent worked for the seller, and the agent with the buyer was a "subagent" of the listing agent.)

Gradually, to accommodate buyers who were skeptical of home conditions, sellers began allowing knowledgeable third parties to make independent evaluations. Over the next decade, those third-party home inspectors would coalesce into a national information-sharing network—the American Society of Home Inspectors.

Still, however, by 1984 the actual number of home inspections being conducted was relatively small, and resistance to inspections by the brokerage community was comparatively large. Real estate agents already were seeing inspectors as "deal killers" who would find problems, exaggerate them, and inform buyers that they weren't getting nearly as good a deal as they should.

Plus, it was worth noting, some inspectors seemed to be working more for themselves than the homebuyer—finding problems and fixing them for a fee. More on that later.

Along Comes *Easton*

So the idea that brokers had some responsibilities to buyers already was established by the time *Easton* came along. Given the times and the anti-big business attitudes of consumers and legislatures, in many ways *Easton* was a decision waiting to happen—and a fairly straightforward one at that. Let's look at what happened:

The Strassburgers owned a home and an adjacent lot in a hilly upscale community in Contra Costa County outside San Francisco. Mudslides were a recurring hazard in the area.

When the home was built, construction workers had to move a large amount of dirt to create a surface flat enough on which to build. The workers, however, did not take care to stabilize the extra dirt that was piled against a hill on the adjacent lot during construction.

As early as 1973, rains had triggered minor mudslides that hit the house. In 1975, a major slide hit the house, resulting in damage. The Strassburgers repaired the damage and also made an effort to repile the dirt against the hill. The following year, 1976, the Strassburgers sold the property to the Eastons.

They never mentioned the mudslides in any documents, nor their efforts to restore the hill.

In 1978, a major mudslide hit the home and virtually destroyed the house. The Eastons sued the Strassburgers, the builders, and the real estate agents, claiming they had the right to know before they bought the house that the hill was dangerous. The trial court found in favor of the Eastons and apportioned 65 percent of the penalties to the Strassburgers for not revealing the truth and 5 percent to the real estate brokers. The real estate brokers appealed, claiming they were deceived by the Strassburgers just as much as the Eastons.

What the high court ruled, however, stunned the industry.

The appeals court held that because real estate agents are licensed professionals, not only did they have a duty to disclose what they knew, they also had a duty "as professionals" to "use their knowledge, skills, and experience" to identify potential defects.

The court said the agents ignored the presence of the dirt pile and the erosion netting that had been placed on the slopes of the hill, as well as the uneven floors in the home that suggested the ground was shifting under the house. The court held that the agents had "an affirmative duty to further investigate such obvious signs of distress," regardless of what the seller disclosed.

In other words, not only were agents obligated to make buyers aware of known defects, they also were obligated to investigate possible problems and disclose those unknown defects.

After *Easton*

Needless to say, the brokerage community reacted in the extreme. How could agents know about defects that weren't disclosed to them? They didn't live in the house, nor were they experts in home construction. If they weren't told of defects by the sellers, how would an agent know the truth?

The brokerage community also realized that the courts had bestowed on sales agents a level of "professionalism" that didn't exist. It knew its agent workforce was not nearly well enough educated to recognize defects, even if they saw them.

Suddenly, company broker/owners could see an endless line of lawsuits stretching out before them. The court, the brokerage industry maintained, had gone way too far. Something had to be done.

So in the aftermath of *Easton,* the real estate brokerage industry exercised its considerable clout in state legislatures nationwide to pass laws to get brokers out from under the liability umbrella. The attack was multipronged, and in many ways continues today.

Companies wanted state legislators to

- limit the broker's liability in cases where a homeowner had not identified defects;
- establish by law exactly what kind of problems must be disclosed, thus excusing both seller and agent from all other defects (and thus ushering in the era of check-off forms);
- raise the level of education required of agents to stay in the business; and,
- most important, try to shift liability from themselves to other professionals. Those "other professionals" were home inspectors.

By and large, those lobbying efforts have met with success. Also, a number of cases since *Easton* have softened its impact considerably.

Today, while most states still charge listing agents with the obligation to disclose observable defects, in most cases they are no longer obligated to second-guess a seller when a seller says there are no problems.

But the courts also appear to be handling those questions on a case-by-case basis.

Shifting Opinions

At the same time that real estate brokerages were trying to get out from under the liability imposed by *Easton*, more consumers and even real estate agents were seeing the need for someone to represent the buyer in the transaction to thwart deceptive sellers. Even as consumers began seeing the need for home inspectors, they also began seeing the need for "buyer agents."

Inside the industry, home inspectors and buyer agents were both considered nuisances. Their purpose seemed to be little more than to nickel and dime deals to death.

Over the years, however, those opinions have changed.

Listing agents (and the courts) have come to see that if home-buyers are represented by their own real estate agents, then the listing agent has fewer legal responsibilities to those buyers. If there are professionals on both sides of the transaction, then each can be an advocate for their own client's best interest.

Also, to be blunt, some brokers, listing agents, and sellers came to see home inspectors as scapegoats. Instead of revealing anything about a home, sellers and agents began listing properties "as is"—essentially claiming they are unaware of any problems. The logic went: Why not just let a buyer have the home inspected and take the chance that the inspector will find all the defects? Theoretically, if the inspector missed something, it would be the inspector's fault, not the seller's fault, and certainly not the listing agent's fault.

Fortunately, however, the courts have seen through that ploy. Most states continue to require sellers to reveal "known defects," even if they are selling a home "as is." In the modern day, the phrase "as is" is interpreted to mean the seller won't pay to repair any defects—but known defects must still be revealed.

Shifting Liability to Inspectors

Clearly, as the industry moved through the 1990s, home inspectors were carrying more weight in terms of liability—and the home inspection industry, growing in both numbers and strength, began to respond. More insurance companies came forward offering Errors and Omissions (E&O) insurance, meaning that in most cases inspectors could be covered if they were sued for damages because they missed something in the inspection.

However, as Alan Carson of Carson Dunlop in Toronto says, the decision whether or not to carry E&O is not an easy one.

"Many home inspectors these days carry E&O insurance, but they won't admit it. They feel like it's an invitation to be sued. Some [consumers] won't feel like they're suing the inspector, just the insurance company."

On the other hand, "Some [consumers] will only hire someone who has E&O," adds Carson, "because they look on the home inspector with E&O as being more professional than those who don't."

E&O is mandatory in some places, but is available *everywhere.* "Most inspectors don't feel like they need it, but they also know that if they get hit by a lawsuit they could be put out of business," Carson says.

Even worse, inspectors could be put out of business whether or not they've done anything wrong because the cost of fighting a lawsuit is so high.

Additionally, it is important to note that it is often cheaper to settle a lawsuit out of court—even if you've done nothing wrong—than to fight the case. The problem with that, of course, is that many real estate agents see a "settlement out of court" as meaning "he must have been guilty." Your business could suffer accordingly.

Inspectors who decide not to carry E&O essentially are hoping that once a consumer's attorney sees they have no deep-pocket insurance company behind them, they will lose interest in the case.

The best defense against legal action, of course, is to avoid it altogether. More states have begun regulating the inspection industry, requiring more classroom education and on-site training before allowing individuals to inspect homes.

And, of course, in an effort to raise the image of the entire industry, various inspector trade organizations have toughened membership requirements. Organizations also began lobbying to ease inspector liability by narrowing the definition of "home inspection," what is included, and what consumers are entitled to if the inspector makes a mistake.

In the recent past, some inspection companies have attempted to limit the extent of their liability to the price of the home inspection. The courts, however, have been inconsistent in upholding those contracts. Some judges have agreed that if a written and signed contract limits recourse to the price of the inspection, then those contracts should be upheld. Other judges have ruled, however, that many consumers don't understand the contracts they are signing and that it is unfair to allow an inspector to simply return his fee if he or she's failed to notice a problem that could cost the client thousands of dollars.

What's Fair

Harry Rosenthal, legal counsel for the American Society of Home Inspectors, believes even now many consumers and real estate agents do not understand what a home inspection truly is: an observation on the condition of the property on the day it was inspected.

"A lot of people believe that since they've had an inspection, the inspector has warranted the property against defects. That's not the case," he says. "All an inspector is giving his client is a general description. That doesn't mean that something won't break tomorrow.

"I've always believed that inspectors accept a huge amount of liability (potentially tens of thousands of dollars) for the fee that they charge (usually only a few hundred dollars). That doesn't make sense. Inspectors are awfully underpaid for the risks they take."

The Need to Get Better

In some ways, the home inspection industry still is recovering from its earliest days when anyone who said he was a home inspector, and could hang up a sign saying he was a home inspector, essentially was a home inspector.

The industry was both unlicensed and unruly. Many of those early participants were unskilled in modern inspector practices, and abuses were rampant. As was mentioned before, it was not unusual for an inspector to discover a problem and at the same time offer to fix it—for a fee. Clearly, the more "problems" an inspector found, the more fix-it fees he could charge. Scams developed rapidly.

As the need to regulate the industry took hold, however, more states began embracing the standards of practice adopted by reputable home inspector organizations that prohibited or delayed inspectors from doing repair jobs. By most accounts, the number of abuses has diminished substantially.

"There is a shakeout going on now," says ASHI's Rosenthal. "There is going to be even more legislation in the future that will continue to force bad inspectors out of the business.

"More state are going to require E&O insurance, and inspectors who can't meet the standards of their carriers are going to be forced out. At the same time, inspections are going to be more uniform, more standard. Consumers will have a better understanding of what a home inspection is.

"The real estate brokers are coming around too. Many are starting to see that a good home inspection keeps them out of trouble. Yes, inspections complicate a lot of deals—but ultimately it's in their own best interest."

CHAPTER 16

Everything Is About Ethics

Why it is important not to lie to your client, and to be careful about who you take money from.

The easiest thing to do is sit at a computer keyboard and type the words "BE ETHICAL." We could fill it in a little more with the words "DON'T LIE TO YOUR CLIENT" and "DON'T EMBELLISH YOUR REPORT." And how about adding the ever popular "LET YOUR CONSCIENCE BE YOUR GUIDE"?

Or maybe we could just leave it at "ETHICS, YOU EITHER GOT 'EM OR YOU DON'T."

The problem is that in one way or another, all those statements oversimplify a complex issue in the home inspection business. Ethical questions are something you are likely to encounter every day of your professional life (although in all honesty, the biggest challenges will come at the very beginning of your career when your standards may not be quite fixed in concrete).

As we went over in Chapter 7, everyone in the deal—the buyer, the seller and the various agents—would like to influence your report. It's up to you make sure that what's in your report is a simple and accurate reflection of the current condition of the home.

But the ethical challenges you are likely to meet go beyond whether to write that the roof leaks "a lot" or "a little," or whether the ceiling fan is or isn't performing up to par.

- What about when you see a problem that you could fix for $100?
- What about referring the buyer (or seller) to a home repair company owned by your brother?
- Or even, is it OK to accept a referral from a real estate agent, knowing full well that agent has a vested interest in how the report comes out?

Consider Yourself a Traffic Light

What most homebuyers are looking for when they hire an inspector is someone to give them either a green light—buy the house, or a red light—don't buy the house. And, of course, what the inspection business really is about is providing shades of cautionary yellow.

It's not your job to say the house is worth the money. Nor is it your job to say it isn't. Your job is only to point out problems, possibilities, and probabilities, and then leave it to the consumer to make the decision.

Home inspector Alan Carson of Toronto-based Carson Dunlop says the thing every new home inspector needs to ask is whether he or she is in business for the long term or "just to make a quick buck."

"If you are in this job for the long term, if you want to do what it takes to survive in the business, you need to represent the house as you see it," he says. "Your loyalty has to be with the house.

"It is easy enough already to make honest mistakes and make misstatements of opinion without worrying about coloring a report one way or the other. At the end of the day, you need to feel that if it comes down to it, some judge or lawyer or mediator or arbitrator can hold your feet to the fire and that you'll be able to say, 'Yes, that's what my report said and here's why I said that . . .'"

And in the end, he says, real estate agents—those who are true professionals—wouldn't have it any other way.

"Real estate agents also are trying to build their reputations," Carson says. "They tend to be successful if they give good service to their clients. They are trying to build their business and their network. And if their clients end up extremely unhappy, they're not going to be in business for long."

Been There, Done That

The good news is that long before you even considered getting into the home inspection business, there were trade organizations comprising many members who already had experienced many of the questions that you can expect in your career. And they have developed answers.

For instance, the American Society of Home Inspectors (ASHI), the National Association of Home Inspectors (NAHI), and the National Association of Certified Home Inspectors (NACHI), have each compiled lists of issues their members face, and have distilled those lists into codes of ethics.

If you join any of those groups, or others, you likely will be encouraged to adhere to their codes.

Mind you, we are not talking about silly stuff here. We're not talking about secret handshakes or decoder rings. Adhering to a Code of Ethics can help do at least two things for you: One, keep you in business; and two, keep you out of court.

- Adhering to a code will keep you in business because you will develop a reputation as a consistent, balanced observer of fact. Consistency is important because markets move from "sellers' markets" to "buyers' markets" and back again. Inspectors who are consistent despite swings in the market are likely to always have work.
- Adhering to a code will keep you out of courts because many states have actually codified trade association codes of

ethics. And it is not unusual for courts to reference industry codes of ethics as the basis for their decisions.

So What Are These Codes?

The ASHI, NAHI, and NACHI codes are similar, but with a few differences—mostly addressing how and whom you should get money from and under what circumstance.

Basically, they each call for you to be fair and honest and objective. Don't discriminate against potential clients on the basis of race, sex, religion, or national origin. And they all say that if the state law differs from the code, follow the state law.

Make sure your report is an accurate reflection of the home: Don't make things sound worse than they are, or better.

In one way or another, the codes also each suggest that you be careful who you deal with. If you deal with disreputable people, either other home inspectors or disreputable real estate professionals, clearly the concern is that images will be tarnished and reputations ruined.

They all warn against trying to be something you're not, or doing tests you're not licensed to do. Do not say a basement is radon-free unless you are trained in determining whether a basement is radon-free; do not claim to be an expert on old wood-burning stoves unless you are an expert on old wood-burning stoves. And don't advertise or promote yourself as an expert in areas where you are not an expert.

Stay within your education, your training, and your experience.

Finally, they all agree that you need to make sure that the only one who sees a copy of your report is the one who paid for it. You should not make a copy available to any real estate agent unless your client says it is OK to provide a copy. Likewise, do not give a copy of the report to the seller just because the seller asks for it. The report belongs to whomever paid for it.

They also all agree, however, that if in the course of your inspection you discover a serious emergency problem—such as a gas leak or major electrical issue—you are obligated to make that concern known immediately to all involved.

These things are relatively obvious.

Less obvious, however, especially to the new home inspector, is the concern over conflict of interest.

Each of the codes recommends against you inspecting a property in which you have a financial interest. For instance, if you are selling a house, do not inspect it and claim you represent the buyer's interests. Lawsuits are made of things like that.

Also, when you inspect a house, know where your fee is coming from and don't accept fees (oh, let's call them "bribes") from other people. You need to be objective on behalf of your client, even if a homeseller on the other side of the table tries to push a pile of cash in your direction. That's not a good way to do business.

Likewise, it's not a good idea to accept jobs where there are strings attached. Agents may say they'll recommend you for additional work, providing your reports read the way the agent wants them to read. That may bring you business (for a while), but it will destroy your credibility over the long term.

Another point is to let your talent do your talking. Your reputation should be good enough to get you referrals and recommendations. Never pay real estate agents or anyone else to get your name onto a "recommended" list.

There is disagreement, however, over whether and how you should recommend other services and whether you should collect referral fees for making those recommendations. You may find, for instance, that there appears to be foundation damage in the basement.

Some groups say you should simply say, "There's damage to the foundation," and then leave it to your client to decide what to do about it.

Others suggest it's OK to say, "There's damage to the foundation, and I know a company that would do a good job of repairing it."

And yet others say it's all right to say, "There's damage to your foundation, I know a company that would do a good job of repairing it, and—by the way—I get a referral fee if you use them."

Each of those answers is legitimate. It's up to you to decide whether one is more legitimate than another. And, clearly, it is still up to clients to decide if they want to hire that company or another one.

The groups generally agree, however, that it is not a good idea to collect a fee from a third-party company without at least disclosing that you're getting it.

There also is concern about whether you should actually bid on doing repairs that you discover.

Both the ASHI and NACHI codes require that their members wait at least one year following an inspection to make repair services available to the client. The feeling is that after a year has lapsed, a buyer has had plenty of time to decide what to do about an issue—the back porch, for instance—and to contact another company if he or she had wanted to do something quickly.

NAHI takes a less prohibitive stance. Its code suggests that the inspector may sell additional products and services, if needed, to the client at the time of the inspection, provided the client is aware of the inspector's financial interest and is given an opportunity to accept or reject the additional fee-based work. Also, the client must be afforded an opportunity to bid out the work to another company. (In some states, inspectors are prohibited from doing any additional fee-based work for a client. Be sure to check your state laws.)

On the Horizon . . .

There remains considerable conversation in the industry about referrals from real estate agents. By some estimates, home inspectors receive as much as 80 percent of their business from agents.

The fear is conflict of interest.

Most agents maintain they want to be able to (and should be able to) direct their clients to the most competent home inspector they can find. Questions arise, however, over what agents consider "competent."

An inspector who never finds problems might be considered extremely competent by some agents and extremely incompetent by others.

Adding intensity to the debate is that very few real estate agents only work one side of the fence. Today, they may represent a buyer in one deal, and tomorrow they may represent a seller in another deal.

If an inspector beats up a home listed by an agent one day, will that agent recommend that inspector to a buyer the next day?

It is an ongoing conversation.

CHAPTER 17

The Organizational You

Sometimes you wanna go where everybody knows your name.

It's Important to Join the Club

There are requirements for and there are benefits of joining an organization of home inspectors. Fees can range from as little as $25 up to several hundred dollars.

But you should join, even if it seems like a costly investment for someone just starting out in the business. It will be worth it.

There are groups like the granddaddy of home inspection organizations–the American Society of Home Inspectors, Inc. (ASHI®)–ranging all the way to very small groups devoted to certain areas such as historic building inspections. There are two groups determined to keep inspectors independent from others in the real estate transaction. And there are even groups that want to train you to get into this business.

You need to know that home inspection can be an isolating profession in terms of opportunities to interact with and learn from your peers. You will spend most of your time competing against them for business in your local area. When you do get a job, you'll be the only inspector there.

Let's face it. The clients you serve—whether buyers or sellers—and their real estate agents expect you to be the expert and more.

So how do you keep up-to-date on everything, and avoid new or continuing problems facing inspectors, when you're spending all your time competing for business and then doing a thorough job?

You join at least one industry organization.

It's a win-win situation. You get to put a new logo, and possibly some impressive initials, on your business card. You can brag that you follow, or exceed, the group's "Standards of Practice." And membership shows you care enough about being a home inspector to join a professional group and continue learning about your industry.

In addition, you'll gain access to valuable information and support, along with an established network and referral opportunities to increase your bottom line. Some groups even offer discounts on everything from training to car rentals.

Joining a group is even more important if you do not belong to a franchise. But even if you do, it never hurts to take advantage of as many opportunities as possible to learn more about your industry and help improve your skills—and your profits.

Reasons to Belong

One sure way for newcomers to increase their credibility in the home inspection industry and in the eyes of the public is to join a professional society, contends F. Jay Schnoor of Professional Home Inspection in La Crescent, Minnesota.

"It helps to give the client assurance that I'm not a fly-by-night guy, but that there is some substance, continuing education, and certifications. I'm a Certified Real Estate Inspector. That's really the highest designation in the industry."

To earn the CRI from the National Association of Home Inspectors (NAHI), Schnoor was required to complete 250 inspections and pass a rigorous exam, and must maintain 16 hours of continuing education annually. Other groups may have different criteria for certification or membership, but all offer the

"**I** think that as a new inspector, it would be important to have the association and credentials behind me. It shows I follow certain standards and there is a code of ethics that I follow," says Schnoor, a mechanical and industrial engineer who turned to home inspecting full-time in 1992. ■

ability to interact with fellow members either online or face-to-face at meetings and at conventions.

Mardi Clissold of Home Critic in Austin, Texas, believes it is extremely important for new inspectors, in particular, to have some venue where they can "toss around ideas." "Out on your own, you don't get to talk to anyone about things you run into," she says.

For Clissold, some of that interplay is available at quarterly meetings with the other inspectors who operate as independent contractors under the Home Critic umbrella.

"Otherwise, I would feel really isolated. I wouldn't be getting the horror stories or the war stories on what's happening out in the field. That's invaluable, especially being in business by myself. Otherwise, I might make a mistake I could have avoided."

Nick Gromicko, founder of the Pennsylvania-based National Association of Certified Home Inspectors (NACHI), agrees and says the Internet also has provided new opportunities for communication through such formats as message boards where inspectors can post e-mails about various topics.

"The Internet has made it much easier. Before, there was no camaraderie in the home inspection business. You could go long months without interacting with other home inspectors," he says.

"Something dramatic could happen, like an important recall, and an inspector wouldn't know about it unless he attended a meeting or bought a periodical. The Internet has changed all that. All inspectors can know about a recall moments after it's posted."

In addition, there are online opportunities for "discussions" about topics of interest to home inspectors. On the NACHI site, for example, there have been many thousands of postings by inspectors in 28 countries and by representatives of other businesses related to the home inspection industry, such as homeowners' insurance companies and home inspection continuing education vendors. One need not be a NACHI member to participate.

"Everyone is welcome and the truth bubbles from the bottom to the top. The Internet has changed everything. Now there is great camaraderie in our industry and inspectors are keeping in touch with the industry," says, Gromicko.

Ralph Wirth of Housing Consultants Inc., in Louisville, Kentucky, says professional home inspection organizations offer another valuable benefit beyond credibility, certification, education, and fellowship—an opportunity to be heard. That can be extremely important during efforts to institute, or increase, regulation of the home inspection industry within a state or local area.

"The only voice you have in the business world is when your united voice comes through your national association," says Wirth.

So find your voice, within your group and within the world, by joining at least one industry group in your local area or your state, or find one with a national, or even international, membership.

As would be expected, there are ardent supporters—and sometimes, ardent opponents—of some of the national groups. Find one that suits your needs and comfort level. Do some research on the Internet and if you have the opportunity, ask other inspectors which group or groups they belong to and why.

In the meantime, here is a sampling of national home inspection organizations for you to consider. States may have their own groups and/or chapters of a national organization.

The American Society of Home Inspectors, Inc.® (ASHI®)

By far the oldest, most generally known home inspection organization, ASHI is a not-for-profit professional society established in 1976 that now claims over 6,000 members and more than 80 chapters in North America.

ASHI Standards of Practice are part of many pieces of state legislation. The group includes on its Web site a description of the regulatory legislation of each state that licenses home inspectors.

ASHI, which has a branding program called the "ASHI Experience," endorses three ways to train new home inspectors: a home training system, two-week hands-on seminars, and classes at community colleges. One need not be a member to take ASHI-endorsed training.

It is one of the more expensive groups to initially join (over $400 in 2004). New and experienced inspectors alike first sign up as a Candidate for a minimum 30-day period of review of their qualifications and/or to take the National Home Inspectors Exam and the ASHI Standards and Ethics exams.

The group has two additional membership levels, and all require a pledge to follow the group's Standards and Code of Ethics, to not engage in real estate activities or to repair homes they inspect. Candidates with Logo may use the ASHI logo if they pass the two exams and ASHI verifies performance of 50 fee-paid inspections "in substantial compliance" with its Standards of Practice. Full Members must submit proof of performance of 250 fee-paid inspections that meet or exceed ASHI standards. After the first year of membership, all must obtain 20 units of continuing education annually.

Member benefits include online discussion groups, access to technical and business resources, lobbying and public relations efforts raising awareness of the industry, a national referral directory, discounts, and various publications.

Consumers may use the Web site to find ASHI inspectors within 150 miles of a zip code; by metropolitan area and neighborhoods; or by name or company. Also offered to consumers: a virtual home inspection to learn more about common problems found by inspectors and a form to rate inspectors.

The American Society of Home Inspectors, Inc.® (ASHI®)
932 Lee Street, Suite 101
Des Plaines, IL 60016
Phone: (800) 759-2820
Fax: (847) 759-1620
www.ashi.org

The National Association of Home Inspectors, Inc. (NAHI)

NAHI, established in 1987 as a nonprofit association, calls itself the "Home Inspector–Friendly Association" and claims more than 1,900 members in 49 U.S. states and Canada. As with ASHI, there are states that reference the NAHI standards in their own legislation and other groups that accept NAHI's Certified Real Estate Inspector exam as part of their membership requirements.

Member benefits include use of the NAHI logo, a newsletter, public relations support, a member e-forum, and listing in the NAHI referral directory.

NAHI offers Associate Membership to new inspectors who have completed a 40-hour comprehensive home inspection training program or 20 full fee-paid inspections. They must submit a copy of a completed full home inspection report that meets NAHI Standards of Practice and Code of Ethics requirements and complete at least eight continuing education units annually.

Inspectors can maintain Associate Member status for up to two years prior to moving to the Regular Member status, which requires a minimum of 100 full fee-paid written home inspections and written confirmation of passing the NAHI Certified Real Estate Inspector, National Home Inspector Exam, or California Real Estate Inspector exam. In addition, Regular Members must complete a minimum of eight continuing education units annually.

NAHI members may earn the CRI (Certified Real Estate Inspector) designation by fulfilling the above requirements, completing 250 fee-paid inspections, and passing an exam. To retain the designation, they must maintain 16 continuing education credits and undergo an annual review of completed home inspection reports.

Consumers using the NAHI Web site may search for NAHI inspectors by entering the zip code of the home to be inspected and choosing a radius of 10, 20, 50, or 100 miles, or they may search by city, state, or country.

National Association of Home Inspectors, Inc.
4248 Park Glen Road
Minneapolis, MN 55416
Phone: (952) 928-4641 or (800) 448-3942
Fax: (952) 929-1318
www.nahi.org

The National Association of Certified Home Inspectors (NACHI)

NACHI says it is a nonprofit organization dedicated to helping home inspectors achieve financial success and inspection excellence. Formed in 1990, it claims over 9,400 members in all 50 states plus 22 countries and has 55 chapters.

NACHI offers both Working and Full Membership categories. Both require passing the three online tests, promising to adhere to the Code of Ethics and Standards of Practice, and, after the first year of membership, completing an average of 18 hours of continuing education annually (attendance at each NACHI chapter meeting contributes 1 hour to the total required). To reach Full Membership, one must have participated in 100 inspections and also retake the Online Inspector Examination annually. Members have access to mediation and arbitration services, and free peer reviews to improve reports, along with discounts and use of the NACHI logo.

NACHI funds the Consumer Home Inspection Hotline to help the homebuying public find certified inspectors and *www.BribeWatch.org,* a consumer advocacy group that reports suspected corruption in both home inspection and construction legislation. In addition, NACHI and its NACHI Foundation formed a fund to "provide disaster relief to **victims of uncertified inspectors.**"

Consumers using the Web site may search for inspectors by entering their zip code and choosing a radius from that zip code of 10, 20, 30, 50, or 100 miles, or they may search by city and state. The consumer is then taken to NACHI's *www.findaninspector.us* site. NACHI also owns the *www.inspectorseek.com site.*

National Association of Certified Home Inspectors
P.O. Box 987
Valley Forge, PA 19482-0987
Phone: (610) 933-4241 (PA)
Fax: (650) 429-2057 (CA)
www.nachi.org

National Academy of Building Inspection Engineers (NABIE)

Established in 1989, NABIE is a nonprofit professional society that accepts only state-licensed professional engineers and registered architects specializing in building inspections. It claims 165 members.

NABIE believes that "those aspects of building inspection which require the application of engineering principles constitute the practice of engineering and should only be performed by licensed professional engineers. Such aspects include but are not limited to the evaluation of commercial, industrial, and institutional building and residential dwellings, regarding the structural, electrical, or mechanical systems."

Member benefits include various publications and a referral directory listing. NABIE is an affinity group of the 70,000-member National Society of Professional Engineers.

NABIE has a Standards of Practice, and its Web site offers consumers the ability to search for NABIE engineers by state and also offers answers to frequently asked questions.

National Academy of Building Inspection Engineers
P.O. Box 520
York Harbor, ME 03911
Phone: (800) 294-7729
Fax: (207) 351-1915
www.nabie.org

The Housing Inspection Foundation (HIF)

HIF says it is "dedicated to the promotion and development of Home Inspection" and claims 4,500 members.

HIF offers a RHI, or Registered Home Inspector, designation to members with at least two years of experience in the home inspection field, or 50 inspections completed. Members are expected to adhere to the group's Code of Ethics and follow its Uniform Home Inspection Standards of Practice.

It also says it offers a CHI, or Certified Home Inspector, to members who have completed 50 home inspections and passed a 100-question open-book test mailed with a free home inspection manual. There is also a continuing education requirement.

Benefits include use of the HIF logo, publications (including a newsletter), and a listing in the annual membership directory.

Consumers may search the Web site for an HIF inspector by state or country.

Housing Inspection Foundation
1224 North Nokomis NE
Alexandria, MN 56308
Phone: (320) 763-6350
Fax: (320) 763 9290
http://iami.org/hif

Groups Developed by Training Programs

National Institute of Building Inspectors® (NIBI®)

The National Institute of Building Inspectors (NIBI) was formed in 1986 to provide professional training and certification. It operates a training facility in New Jersey and also offers online courses. It claims 350 members in the United States and Canada.

NIBI Certified Inspectors are required to complete the NIBI training course, satisfactorily pass its exam or the National Home Inspectors Exam, complete at least 50 home inspections and submit the addresses, submit reports from two inspections for review, and carry Errors and Omissions liability insurance. They also must participate in the NIBI Continuing Education Program and retake a certification exam annually.

NIBI posts a Code of Ethics on its Web site and offers a members-only message board.

Consumers may search the NIBI Web site by state, and then view listings of NIBI Certified Inspectors by county.

National Institute of Building Inspectors
424 Vosseller Avenue
Bound Brook, NJ 08805
Phone: (888) 281-6424
Fax: (732) 469-2138
www.nibi.com

American Institute of Inspectors® (AII)

AII, formed in 1989 as a nonprofit corporation, claims more than 300 members. It offers training courses for new and experienced inspectors.

The group offers Associate Membership to anyone who pays the fee. Certified Membership requires successful completion of AII training, or passing another recognized certification exam, submitting three recent inspection reports for review, and attending an AII new-member seminar at an AII Conference. Certified members receive logo use, access to an Electronic Mail Hotline and a weekly newsletter, and a Standards of Practice and Code of Ethics.

Consumers may search for AII inspectors by zip code.

American Institute of Inspectors
1421 Esplanade Ave., Suite 7
Klamath Falls, OR 97601
Phone: (800) 877-4770
Fax: (541) 273-1780
www.inspection.org

American Inspectors Society (AIS)

Established in 1971 to "promote excellence within the home inspection industry," AIS offers a lifetime membership to those who complete its training program of classroom and in-the-field instruction, self-study, and oral and written tests. Members must abide by the Standards of Practice and Code of Conduct.

Consumers may find AIS members by clicking on a state to get a name but then must call (770) 695-2894 for additional information.

> American Inspectors Society
> P.O. Box 429
> Maysville, GA 30558
> Phone: (770) 416-9877
> *www.homeinspectortraining.com*

National Association of Real-estate Inspection & Evaluation Services (NARIES™)

NARIES, a for-profit corporation established in 1999, says it is open to everyone and includes among its members inspectors, appraisers, real estate professionals, and others.

It is an outgrowth of Aries Co. (Architectural Review, Inspection & Evaluation Schools), which offers correspondence home inspector training. NAREIS offers a Standards of Practice and Code of Ethics, along with publications and logo use.

> National Association of Real-estate Inspection & Evaluation Services (NARIES)
> P.O. Box 532
> Edmonds, WA 98020
> Phone/Fax: (800) 583-5821
> *http://www.naries.org/*

Groups with a Niche

Historic Building Inspectors Association

Formed in 2003 for inspectors actively involved in dealing with historic preservation, this group counts only a handful of members but says it has rejected more members than it has approved.

A member must pass either the NHIE or the NAHI CRI exam, complete at least 200 fee-paid inspections, maintain valid state or municipal licenses, and maintain 16 hours of continuing education requirements annually. In addition, two inspection reports on buildings constructed before 1925 must be submitted for review.

> Historic Building Inspectors Association
> PO Box 201
> Springtown, PA 18081
> (610) 346-7880, Ext. 3
> *http://inspecthistoric.org/*

Independent Home Inspectors of North America (IHINA)

IHINA says its primary mission is to help alert prospective homebuyers to the potential, or inherent, conflict of interest when a person/agent selling a house also recommends the person/inspector to inspect it for the prospective buyer. IHINA claims 125 members in 24 states and Canada.

It believes state and provincial real estate licensing laws should be amended by adding a "firewall" between real estate agents and home inspectors, similar to that enacted by Massachusetts to prohibit real estate agents, other than buyer's agents, from "directly" recommending a home inspector.

IHINA members sign a "No Conflict of Interest Pledge" that they will not actively solicit real estate agents for client leads and will follow the group's Code of Ethics. The Web site has various photos and articles of interest to home inspectors, along with links to states that have, or are considering, home inspection legislation.

Consumers may locate IHINA inspectors by clicking on a state's name on the Web site.

> Independent Home Inspectors of North America
> 643 Broadway, Suite 155
> Saugus, MA 01906
> Phone: (781) 231-0236
> *www.independentinspectors.org*

Foundation for Independent Home Inspection (FIHI®)

The Foundation is a nonprofit association of home inspectors who pledge "to put the interest of their clients above all else." It was formed in 2003, primarily for registered engineers.

Members must promise "to not be influenced by builders, mortgage companies, REALTORS®, relocation organizations, sellers or anyone else with an interest in the outcome of a home inspection," and to follow the Standards of Practice and Code of Ethics.

Benefits include use of the FIHI® logo, listing on the Web site, and monthly training with an optional test sheet that can be returned for one hour of continuing education of the 12 required annually.

> Foundation for Independent Home Inspection
> PO Box 802
> Emmaus, PA 18049-0802
> Phone: (866) 488-2721
> *http://fihi.info/*

CHAPTER 18

You're Involved in Politics

Whether you want to be or not,
legislatures across the land are tinkering with
your business.

Y es, of course, you don't want to get involved in politics. We don't blame you one bit.

As a new home inspector you have plenty to worry about just trying to get your business off the ground. The last thing you want to think about is what's going on at the state capital.

Couldn't agree with you more.

Be that as it may, it might be a good idea for you to right now—and from time to time throughout your business life—check in with your local legislators to find out if your career is on their agenda.

Surprise! It may be.

Yes, this doesn't seem like the right time to be bringing up politics. But you do need to understand that while you're working to get into this business, there are some people working to keep you out.

Don't take it personally.

The truth is, even as there is a shortage of home inspectors in the country, and even as business tends to be booming, there are people who got into this business ten years ago who are going to be driven out in the next few years. Even more interesting is that if someone with your exact credentials were to come knocking on the industry's door a year from now, they may not be let in. They may not be considered good enough.

What's happening is that the home inspection business, like many other services, is working very hard to improve its image. It is trying to prove it deserves the public's trust. It wants consumers to be assured that they will get the kind of quality they expect when they hire a home inspector and pay their money.

For its part, the industry wants to demonstrate that it is a profession, not just a trade. The best way to do that is to make sure that educational requirements are so rigorous that incompetent people won't be able to get into the business in the first place, and marginal people already in the business will be forced to leave.

In time, this could affect you. You need to try to stay ahead of the wave, and that means knowing when the waves are coming. Congratulations. You're now involved in politics.

Raising the Bar

The major trade associations believe that by the end of the decade, probably every state will have some kind of licensing law for home inspectors. But even if your state already is among those that have regulation—and even if you and your peers consider that regulation to be perfect—you are going to find that the occupants of the state capitol building believe there is no law they can't make better.

And they'd probably be right. Nothing is sacrosanct. The problem is that every new sentence they add to the law could change your job a little—or a lot.

Texas is a perfect example.

In 1985 Texas became the first state in the nation to register home inspectors. Prior to that, the state realized the rankest of amateurs could hang a sign saying he was an inspector and that consumers would come along and believe him. Even worse, those consumers would start basing a large portion of their buy/don't-buy decisions on what those "inspectors" had to say.

And if the inspector proved to be wrong? If the roof actually did leak? Oops. The inspector literally walked away, and the consumer was stuck with an unexpected bill—sometimes a huge one.

Nevertheless, by most accounts the earliest Texas law was more loophole than law. But over a period of years it was successively strengthened until now it is considered one of the strongest licensing laws in the country. But not everyone is satisfied yet.

In the beginning Texas had one fundamental method to become a home inspector:

- Take a certain number of classroom hours covering the basics of an inspection.
- Find an existing inspector who would bring you on (sponsor you) as an apprentice and show you the ropes for a few years.
- After completing a certain number of supervised inspections, you would take the final state inspector exam.
- After that, you would be sponsored into the business.

At that point, you could open your own company and begin to take on your own apprentices. The cycle could begin again.

It was not long, however, until that process proved problematic. Existing home inspectors were proving reluctant to sponsor new people into the industry. Why? They didn't want the competition. After a while sponsors became so hard to come by that the state had to come up with an alternative path to licensure.

So, it developed a second method of becoming an inspector called "Fast Track":

- Take the basic course.
- Take an additional 60 hours of instruction.
- Pass the final exam.

And you were in.

The problem with Fast Track, state officials conceded later, was that pretty soon up to 85 percent of people in the pipeline to become inspectors were using the Fast Track method. They were being approved, even though they may never have inspected a house.

Again, that made state officials nervous. So in 2004 the state came back with another version of the law: Instead of just taking an additional 60 hours of classroom work, prospective inspectors now had to take 320 hours of classroom work—all of it in very specific categories such as roofing systems, HVAC, foundations, electrical, and so forth.

The point is that even if your state already has a licensing law, don't get too cozy thinking that's all you'll ever have to deal with. What one legislator sees as "refining" the law could very well put another person, an inspector, out of business. You need to be on guard if you want to protect you.

Most changes in licensing law are far less sweeping than the Texas example, however, which means that rather than having your wallet and your enthusiasm crushed in a single blow, the government will drain you slowly.

For instance, what if a majority of legislators believe home inspectors need to know more about foundation systems?

They'll amend the state's licensing law and require that all home inspectors get an additional four hours of education—and you will have to comply within the next two years.

The course itself is going to cost you at least a few hundred dollars. Odds are you will have to travel to wherever the course is being taught, which will mean the expense of the round trip, and possibly a hotel for the night.

And don't forget that while you are spending between a few hundred and a thousand dollars to take this course and remain licensed, you are also missing a couple of days of work where you could have been earning fees.

Just a cost of doing business? Of course, and all industries have them.

The idea is that if your state legislature is going to hold your wallet hostage, then you need to make sure that four-hour course in foundations is necessary. It's up to you to make sure that every dime you spend is a dime well spent.

And the questions won't just involve education.

It could be changes in Errors and Omissions insurance requirements. Is it mandatory? (It is in many states.) How much coverage are you going to be required to carry? At how high a price?

Or maybe the question will concern whether you can accept "incentive bonuses" from people like locksmiths or security companies for sending them business. In the old days, taking money for sending people business was called a *kickback*. (Bad.) But today some call it *synergy*. (Good.) (In some states, however—again, with Texas among those leading the way—home inspectors are obligated to disclose in writing whether they have "synergy" with someone else in the deal and how much "synergy" they are receiving or paying out. There are forms that must be given to the client showing where the money is flowing—be it sprinkler installation workers or roofing contractors.)

Maybe the issue will be reciprocity. As an inspector, you know that houses are pretty much constructed the same from one state to another, the problems they develop are pretty much the same from one state to another, and certainly consumers are basically the same from one state to another. Yet you, the inspector, cannot simply step over a state line and inspect a home because the licensing laws may be dramatically different. Should you be able to cross a state border to inspect houses? OK, but should people from other states be allowed to come into your state to inspect houses? Hmmm . . . .

Or as a state goes through and establishes by law what a home inspection must cover, what happens when it decides to add something else? Again, will more and different education be required? Will you have to buy new and expensive special tools?

If you are not involved in the legislative process to help shape, resist, or embrace the changes coming in the business, then you are going to be reduced to having the legislature tell you how you're going to spend your money.

Trade Association Backup

In the last chapter, of course, we urged you to join one of the major home inspection trade associations that are growing around the country, or a state group. One of the chief reasons for you to join is because those associations have more clout in your state's capital than you have on your own.

Currently, it's safe to say that in most common matters, the trade groups are in agreement. They will disagree, however, on issues such as whether and how inspectors may accept referrals from real estate agents. They will occasionally differ on questions like how many supervised inspectors constitute enough for someone to open their own business. They may disagree on how many classroom hours are appropriate or the nature of the state licensing exam.

Eventually, all these things become pocketbook issues.

Because ASHI was the first home inspection trade group to form, it was the first to influence legislators around the country. As a result, some state laws have written the ASHI Code of Ethics into their state laws or referenced them in some other way as the industry's benchmark for performance.

Only in recent years have the other trade associations gained enough strength to forward their own model laws to regulate the industry and seek to intrude on ASHI's legislative clout.

Again, bottom-line:

It's not enough for you to just join a trade association and silently send in your dues. You do have a vested interest in how your industry grows and develops, and you need to be interested in what reforms it backs and what reforms it doesn't. You do have a vested interest in what kinds of laws are enacted to limit the way you do business, or even enhance it.

The best way of knowing whether your industry is in peril is to become involved in committees that are asking those questions.

And Then There Are the Feds

Right now the federal government is not in the home inspection regulating business, and most people believe they don't want the Feds in the home inspection regulating business.

But one of the more interesting developments in recent times has been the mandatory inspection of properties in which consumers are getting loans underwritten by FHA or other government programs.

Those inspections, however, are supposed to be done by appraisers, not inspectors.

The appraisal trade associations have cried foul, saying they don't want to do inspections. And the home inspection organizations have argued appraisers are not trained to make rigorous inspections.

And the government has backed off some, saying that if an appraiser's cursory inspection finds problems, then the buyer should be referred to a true home inspector.

What some people worry about, however, is what will happen if the government ultimately decides to make true home inspections mandatory on all FHA houses. That might sound good to you, and it certainly will mean a lot of work for everyone.

But it's also going to mean that the Feds will start setting standards for what they feel a home inspection should include. Those standards may or may not clash with what state laws say a home inspection should include.

Who would win that battle? More importantly, who would lose it? Would you end up having to train for two sets of standards, a state standard and a federal one?

And if you think working with the state bureaucracy is bad, wait until you have to deal with a federal bureaucracy.

The Challenges Ahead

The real estate business already has survived (more or less) mold and asbestos. But you can be sure there are more challenges coming.

In addition to whether a house works as it should, your clients may very likely also want to know whether it could be hazardous to their health.

Their degree of concern may be linked to recent news stories about one issue or another being harmful to the occupants of a house and/or destroying the house itself. Chemicals used in insulation have been a big thing, and even the paint used on venetian blinds has come under question.

How many times have we read about children being evacuated from schools—and employees from buildings—because of so-called sick building syndrome? What's real and what's hysteria remains a question. Clearly, however, there are such things as Legionnaires' Disease that can develop quite suddenly and be quite lethal.

Also, sometimes consumers read about a lawsuit (or several) filed by homeowners claiming damage or negative health effects. Mold, for example, has become a well-known environmental concern even though mold has existed since the dawn of time. Other issues receiving a great deal of attention in recent years include radon, asbestos, lead-based paint, and synthetic stucco.

You will meet clients who are overly concerned about potential hazards from these and other things and some who are completely unaware that they probably should be. Fortunately, in the vast majority of cases, these issues aren't enough to make a home too dangerous to inhabit. Either a problem does not exist or it can be controlled so there is no harm to the occupants or the house.

Many of the things the modern consumer is worried about are not included in state or trade association standards of practice for a home inspection. Instead, they are considered specific enough to produce a recommendation for a more intensive examination by a trained expert (which could be you offering an additional service for a fee—see the next chapter). Hopefully, you have heard about some during your training. There will be others that could develop into more prominent issues.

You are likely to be asked about them at some point and you may encounter them during an inspection. Depending on where you are, some have been issues for some time while others are just beginning to appear on the radar screen.

Here is a look at some of the continuing issues you may encounter.

Asbestos becomes dangerous only if disturbed because the tiny fibers can become airborne and, if inhaled into the lungs, can lead to cancer and other significant health problems. Asbestos is common in homes built before the late 1970s, and has been primarily used in insulation and as a fire retardant. Common uses include pipe and furnace insulation materials, asbestos shingles, millboard, textured paints and other coating materials, and floor tiles. Asbestos can be verified only under a microscope. Precautions are necessary to obtain samples. Some states require that asbestos inspectors be licensed. The government's information site is *http://www.epa.gov/asbestos/*.

Carbon monoxide (CO) gas is invisible, odorless, and can be deadly within minutes. Problems occur with improper installation, venting, or maintenance of appliances fueled with natural gas, liquefied petroleum (LP gas), oil, kerosene, coal, or wood. An inspector could check for blockages, corrosion, partial and complete disconnections, and loose connections. Many consumers are now installing carbon monoxide detectors, which sound an alarm before potentially life-threatening levels of CO are reached, but lower levels also can cause health problems and flulike symptoms. The government's information Web site is *http://www.epa.gov/iaq/co.html.*

Electric and magnetic fields (EMF) are invisible lines of force that surround any electrical device, including power lines, electric wiring, and electric equipment. Some studies have suggested a possible link between exposure to power-frequency EMF and certain types of cancer. Other studies found no link. Clients may ask about EMF, particularly if a house is located near high-voltage transmission lines. Meters can measure EMF. The magnetic fields result from the flow of current through wires and cannot be blocked by most materials, but they rapidly become weaker with distance from the source. The National Institutes of Health Web site is *http://www.niehs.nih.gov/emfrapid/home.htm.*

Formaldehyde is widely used in the manufacture of building materials and household products and can be emitted by unvented fuel-burning appliances such as gas stoves and kerosene space heaters. Formaldehyde emits a colorless pungent-smelling gas that can cause respiratory problems and possibly cancer. New homes (mobile and conventional) tend to have higher formaldehyde levels due to a large amount of new building materials. Emissions generally decrease as products age. The emission rate is accelerated by heat and may depend on the humidity level. Also, **Urea-formaldehyde (UF)** resin is found in several pressed wood products inside a home such as particleboard, hardwood plywood paneling, and medium density fiberboard used for cabinets and furniture tops. UF foam insulation was popular in the 1970s until it was learned that it results in relatively high indoor concentrations of formaldehyde. Since 1985 the government has set formaldehyde emission rates from plywood and particleboard used in building prefabricated and mobile homes. The government's Web site is *http://www.epa.gov/iaq/formaldehyde.html.*

Lead-based paint is a hazard only if it is peeling, chipping, or cracking. Lead paint has been outlawed in the United States since 1978, but the government believes it remains in three-fourths of the housing in our country. It is especially toxic to children and pets. The government requires that homesellers disclose information about lead paint in their houses. A lead paint inspection—which some states regulate—can include a visual examination of the condition and location of the paint, lab tests of samples, surface dust tests, and use of a portable X-ray fluorescence (XRF) machine. The government's information site is *http://www.epa.gov/opptintr/lead/*.

Mold and mildew (two words for the same thing) are simple plants, of the group known as fungi, that grow on surfaces when the relative humidity is high. Mold can cause discoloration, odor problems, and deterioration of building materials, and result in health problems inside a house. Although necessary for the breakdown of dead organic matter since time began, health concerns from indoor mold exposure and lawsuits have pushed it into the limelight in recent years. Molds reproduce by means of tiny spores that are invisible to the naked eye and float through the air, landing on wet surfaces to grow. There are many types of mold, but none grow without water or moisture. It can be removed with proper cleaning (and elimination of the source of moisture). The government's Web site is: *http://www.epa.gov/iaq/molds/moldguide.html*.

Polybutylene (PB) plumbing installed between Jan. 1, 1978, and July 31, 1995, was the subject of a class action lawsuit that led to a billion-dollar fund to repair or replace leaking PB plumbing systems and yard service lines. PB plumbing was commonly installed in mobile homes, apartments, and other low-cost forms of housing in the 1970s and 1980s. Manufacturers estimate as many as six million housing units contain PB pipes. For more information, see *http://www.pbpipe.com*.

Radon is an odorless, invisible, and radioactive gas produced by the natural breakdown of uranium in soil, rock, and water, and is believed to be the second-leading cause of lung cancer. The government recommends all homes be tested for radon, which moves up through the ground to the air and into homes through cracks and other holes in the foundation, and through well water. It is estimated that 1 of every 15 homes has high radon levels. The government's Web site is *http://www.epa.gov/radon/*.

Synthetic stucco, also known as *exterior insulation and finish systems* or *EIFS*, consists of an adhesive, a Styrofoam-like insulation layer, fiberglass mesh, a base coat, and a durable finish coat—all treated with chemicals to make them hard. It is designed to keep water out and energy in, and it is cheaper than stucco. However, problems occur when moisture seeps in and becomes trapped under the siding, rotting wood beneath it. Some say it never should have been applied over wood building materials, only more durable ones such as brick and stone. It became popular in the 1980s but with more use, more problems began coming to light. Synthetic stucco is soft and sounds hollow when tapped, compared to traditional stucco that sounds solid and is hard and brittle. The EIFS industry Web site is *http://www.eima.com/*.

Things to Come

Here are some areas you should be aware of that may become of increasing concern in the future.

Changes in housing construction methods. Innovations will continue in housing construction, and inspectors will need to be aware of them. For example, inspecting a house assembled on a foundation after being built within a huge facility will require expertise to determine if it has been put together correctly.

On some tracts getting ready to be developed, builders have started using on-site robotic manufacturing plants in which the house design is fed into a computer and a house is spit out the other end. Are these houses better or worse than stick-built homes?

Changes in building products. Building products also will continue to change, and inspectors should be aware of how those changes can affect an entire house. For example, a new type of wooden joist that looks like a steel I-beam has a loading maximum that might not be exceeded if carpet is installed, but what happens if it is replaced by heavier ceramic tile?

Other premanufactured products replacing those previously built during standard construction also may have less margin for error. In addition, some people are raising questions about compounds used as deck preservatives that contain arsenic.

Chemists are coming up with better insulations. In fact, one company has developed an insulation out of soybeans that it says rivals anything already on the market. There are light-sensitive films being built into window glass that can be tuned to allow in more or less light.

The problem is, as we've seen with everything from recalled drugs to recalled automobiles, it could be years before we really know how well these innovations stand up—whether they do more good than harm, how long they'll last, and how hard they'll be to repair or replace.

Roof certifications. More and more lenders, including the Federal Housing Administration, are requiring that roofs be certified for at least two more years of life before they will issue a loan.

More Study

As you can see, for good or ill, the federal government is thoroughly involved in researching the products that go into homes, as is the National Association of Home Builders' Research Center. Also, something called the "National Center for Healthy Housing" has been funded by the Centers for Disease Control and Prevention in Atlanta to develop a training center for people like you where you can learn more about detecting problems in the home environment.

What's obvious is that more concerns will rise and fall in the future as more new products and methods are introduced.

On the other side, however, there is a growing body of people who contend that science has gone mad and that lawyers are making millions because of it.

Some people insist that homes haven't changed all that much over the years, but our ability to test for problems has gone up considerably. The "bad" things that have been in homes forever continue to be there, but only now are we able to detect them, publicize them, and file lawsuits over them.

Home inspectors who choose to specialize can easily be drawn into some of these issues—and some of them are likely to be very lucrative.

It will just be a matter of training.

CHAPTER 20

What Else Can You Do?

With all the skills you have, all you need is a little imagination to come up with a raft of different ways to serve the marketplace.

Once you've explained to your client what a home inspection involves—an objective visual examination of a house's physical structure and primary systems from top to bottom—you may find your client wants more.

That can be good news for you and your bank account.

Due to the fact that a traditional home inspection is a general overview, there very well may be areas where your client has some particular concerns that are outside of the scope of your inspection.

You may be willing to include them without an extra charge. But some of the things are going to take more time and more specialized education than the general inspection. Remember, you are in business to sell your expertise. Don't give it away.

Some of these services require taking a course or two. Some states specify how much training you are required to have, what the specific inspection must include, and that you be licensed. In other cases, it may simply be a matter of you buying a test kit and using it. Check with your state and local licensing agencies.

Don't forget that consumers and real estate agents prefer one-stop shopping. Buying a house is a huge investment. No one wants any surprises afterward, unless they're good ones. Offering extra services will be appreciated and will lead to more business for you and increased peace of mind for the client.

In addition, there is definitely a market for other types of inspections separate from the common add-ons—like septic or termite—to the traditional home inspection.

Former ASHI President Stephen Gladstone of Stamford, Connecticut, believes that anyone who acquires the skills of a home inspector can build his or her career in any number of directions, with more possibilities evolving all the time.

"You can contract with condo associations to inspect units on a routine basis," he says. While individuals are responsible for their own units, condos have common systems such as roofs, heating and air-conditioning, and plumbing that all need to be checked out periodically. "A lot of condo associations want to make sure the building managers are taking care of things. An inspector can tell them."

Likewise, Gladstone sees a future for inspectors who specialize in new home sales. Who would hire an inspector to look at a brand new home? *The builder.*

"Many times work is being done by subcontractors, but after the home is finished, the builder takes responsibility. Builders would be smart to hire inspectors after every phase of a home's construction is completed. If there are problems, it's best to attack them then—not later, when someone has moved in."

It makes economic sense, he says. "When a consumer discovers a problem, they call the builder back to fix it. The average call-back costs the builder $600—and a builder could be called back several times just in the first year. Builders can save thousands if they'd have their homes inspected in phases."

He also sees a future in "forensic diagnostics."

And working with older persons.

"You have older people who have lived in their house for 20 years. They may have no intention of selling, but they haven't

> **"P**eople walk into their house and smell something and they're not sure what to do. An inspector can go out and use his eyes, nose, and detective skills to figure out what's wrong. You could charge whatever you want," says Gladstone. ■

been up in the attic for years, or looked down in the crawlspace. It would make sense for them to have an inspector on retainer just to come out and look at the house every year or so just to make sure that maintenance needs are pointed out, to make sure there are no safety hazards, make sure the filters are changed on the heating systems and that things that need caulk get caulked and things that need to be sealed get resealed.

"It would be routine maintenance—like getting your oil changed every 3,000 miles."

It should go without saying that if you offer ancillary services, and have taken the time to learn how to provide them, make sure you list them in your marketing materials.

And if there are areas where the client wants more checking done, and you just don't possess that expertise, an option is to work out an arrangement with someone who does. That way, the business goes through you, and you are providing the one-stop shopping experience desired by the consumer.

Some specialized inspection areas you could consider offering (and advertising)

Environmental Inspections Often Requested

Asbestos—State or local governments may require training or certification to check for this material, commonly used in a variety of construction materials for insulation and as a fire retardant, but dangerous if disturbed and inhaled into the lungs. It is commonly found in older homes, in pipe and furnace insulation materials, asbestos shingles, millboard, textured paints and other coating materials, and floor tiles. Asbestos professionals take samples of suspected material, assess its condition, and advise what corrections are needed and who is qualified to make them.

Carbon Monoxide—Testing to determining if harmful levels of carbon monoxide are being released by fuel-burning appliances: oil and gas furnaces, gas water heaters, gas ranges and ovens, gas dryers, gas or kerosene space heaters, fireplaces, and wood stoves. Problems occur if they are not properly installed, vented, or maintained. Carbon monoxide cannot be seen or smelled, but it can kill in minutes.

EIFS (Exterior Insulation and Finish Systems)—EIFS, also generally known as *synthetic stucco,* is checked for possible moisture intrusion that can lead to rot. The inspector examines the application and condition, and may remove the siding to determine if there is a problem.

Lead Paint—Although banned in 1978, lead paint remains in an estimated 75 percent of the nation's housing. Federal regulations require that sellers disclose any information about the lead paint in a pre-1978 home and that sales contracts give buyers ten days to check for lead hazards. Buyers also receive the EPA Lead Hazard Information Pamphlet, "Protect Your Family from Lead in Your Home." Inspectors look for lead paint that is peeling, chipping, or cracking because lead exposure causes permanent nervous system damage. Some inspectors offer a swab test, which involves a chemical that indicates the presence of lead, but a special device is required to check the entire home.

Mold—Mold and mildew are names given to thousands of species of fungi that grow in damp areas of wood, paper, carpet, and food and can cause deterioration and illness. An inspection identifies the source, and may include collecting samples for analysis, either from the air or a visible area. Specialized training is available and may be required.

Radon Inspection—Your state may require certification or licensing before you can perform various levels of testing for radon—a common naturally occurring odorless gas believed to cause cancer. The federal government no longer certifies inspectors, but radon proficiency programs are offered by the National Radon Safety Board and the National Environmental Health Association. Results are used to determine if remediation is necessary.

Note: A radon test kit or equipment must be left undisturbed in the closed-up, habitable area of a home for a specific length of time. That means a second trip to retrieve it and getting it to a lab for testing. It is more time-consuming (and adds travel costs) for an inspector.

Water Quality Testing—This involves correctly collecting samples from homes with a municipal water supply, well, or surface water and sending them to a lab for analysis. Clients might be concerned about such substances as lead, coliform bacteria, arsenic, water hardness, radon, MTBE (methyl-t-butyl ether), and so forth. There are various levels of testing.

Prelisting—These inspections are becoming more common and serve two purposes: giving the seller the option to correct any problems and having ready proof of the house's condition available to other potential buyers.

Septic—Inspecting the components of a home's onsite wastewater treatment system, or private septic system, includes looking for signs of leakage and odor. State or local communities may specify the extent of the inspection.

Single Components—These can vary. One example is a roof inspection, where you would either get on the roof or go to the edge of the roof to examine the condition of the roof surface material, look for signs of leaks (including examining ceilings directly under the roof surface), and check the roof drainage system.

Swimming Pool and Spas—Because recreation equipment is not generally part of a home inspection, this involves a visual examination of pool or spa equipment, installation, the electrical supply, and the pool liner, and running the equipment.

Termites/Pests—A visual inspection of the entire readily accessible exterior and interior, including basements and crawlspaces, for evidence of wood-destroying insects and organisms. The attic may be inspected in regions where drywood termites are prevalent but the house has no basement or crawlspace. Licensing or certification is often required.

Well Inspections—May include elements of water quality testing, as well as checking for proper well construction in relation to specific codes and examining well flow and capacity. Training programs are available. State regulations may apply.

Specific Inspection Areas

Commercial Building—An evaluation of the major systems and visible structural components of such commercial buildings as apartment complexes, office buildings, retail stores, and warehouses. Generally, a review of the HVAC (heating, ventilation, and air-conditioning) equipment also is included.

Energy Efficiency Analysis of New/Existing Homes—This is used to establish an energy rating or identify areas where major energy usage improvements can be made.

Home Checkup/Maintenance—Inspections to evaluate the condition of a home to find small problems before they become big ones, to teach homeowners how to maintain a home and/or to get advice before beginning a major renovation or improvement project. Be innovative. You can be on an annual retainer or even charge a "subscription" fee.

Home Warranty—Inspections conducted prior to the end of a home warranty could reveal problems that should be remedied before expiration.

Insurance—Inspections may be required to obtain insurance. In Florida, where there are concerns about homes near beaches, inspectors may offer a four-point inspection of only the roof and the plumbing, HVAC (heating, ventilation, and air conditioning), and electrical systems.

New Construction—These inspections are conducted throughout the construction process, documenting the quality and completeness of each construction phase, or at the predelivery stage.

Additional Inspection Areas

Disaster—Under a contract with FEMA (Federal Emergency Management Agency), the private Partnership for Response and Recovery (*www.parrinspections.com*) hires inspectors to go into declared natural disaster areas and collect information FEMA needs before sending grants to owners and renters whose homes were severely damaged but who have inadequate or no insurance coverage. Training is required. Inspectors sign 30-day contracts.

Expert Witness—An attorney or a homeowner may hire the inspector if there is a question of faulty or negligent work by a contractor or tradesperson or another home inspector. The problem is documented, usually through a full inspection, a written report with supporting pictures, research of local building codes, and testimony in court.

Special Investigations—Clients may hire you to find the source of a specific problem related to their home, such as where a rattling noise is coming from or why there is an odor in their basement.

CHAPTER 21

The High-Tech Home of the . . .

Well, actually, the home of the future is already here.

T he great thing is that this is the best time ever to get into the home inspection business. If you had jumped in yesterday, you would have learned way too many bad habits and would have become way too set in your ways. And if you had waited until tomorrow, you would have been way too far behind to ever catch up (and capitalize) on what's going on in the housing business.

Fortunately, however, today is perfect. There are exciting times ahead and you should be involved.

Every year in North America there are close to 2 million new housing units sold and, according to industry statistics, since the late 1990s almost half of those have been built with the idea that consumers would be installing high-tech gadgets.

In many cases, the wiring for those gadgets has been preinstalled. In many new homes, it's already inside the walls, whether the consumer takes advantage of it or not.

Today, those houses increasingly are moving into the resale market. Home inspectors are seeing strange black boxes in basements and closets with wires running out of them. In ever greater numbers, potential homebuyers are turning to their inspectors asking, "What does that thing do and how do I work it?" (And "Is it working the way it should?")

Currently, the Standards of Practice of all the major home inspection organizations say you should not be required to examine high-tech wiring and high-tech gadgetry as part of the basic home inspection. (Which is a good thing, since there probably aren't more than a handful of inspectors anywhere who could do a proficient job of it.)

On the other hand, in the gap between where the "basic" home inspection ends and where consumer questions end, there is potential to offer additional services that could add value to the inspection—*and* to your bank account.

Even better, you will be one of the first in the field.

Not Your Father's House (But He Could Live There)

Briefly, a lot of what's happening in the housing industry today stems from a collision of two separate phenomena: No. 1, corporations and consumers have fallen in love with the Internet and all the things it can do for them. And No. 2, the aging Baby Boomer generation is heading into its 60s and sociologists are finding Boomers want to live independently at home for as long as they can.

Because of No. 1, corporations increasingly are finding ways, via the Internet, to help consumers access their homes. Either sitting at their computers at work or using cell phones in their cars, they are able to send a signal via the Net back to their house to turn up the heat or turn on the lights. They are able to check home security cameras, and even to preheat the oven. There are gadgets out there that will allow pet owners to trigger a faucet next to Fluffy's water dish to make sure the cat has enough to drink. And that doesn't begin to take into account the wide-screen, high-definition televisions and audio devices that can send sound to any room in the house or back to the swimming pool, or the ability to turn off all the lights in the house and set the alarm system from the bed just before you go to sleep.

Because of No. 2—aging parents who want to continue their independent lifestyles—university research labs have developed new, noninvasive monitoring technologies that can periodically check an elderly occupant's heart rate and breathing. Sensors built into the home will report what the person has in the refrigerator to make sure diets are maintained. The house, ultimately, will be able to remind the occupant to take medicines at the appropriate times—and which pills to take. If issues suddenly arise, like a sudden change in blood pressure, the house itself will be able to alert emergency teams and simultaneously report concerns to the homeowner's physician.

The future is going to be a great place to be.

Yeah, So . . .

According to Jason Knott, head of the Electronic House publishing group in Boston, which is on the cutting edge of much of what is going on, what is powering the "home of the future" is "structured wiring" that can be built into the modern home.

"Think of a house like a car," he says. "In the future, buying a new house without structured wiring will be like buying a car without an engine."

Although who knows what that engine may be in the future, structured wiring today is generally defined as two Cat-5 wires (high-speed telephone lines) and two RG-6 wires (audio/video cable) bundled into a single wrapped wire and run throughout the house. The bundled wire will emerge at "drops," similar in appearance to electrical outlets, that will be located throughout the home.

These bundled outlets will mean that high-tech devices—cable TVs, computers, stereos, and so forth—will be able to plug into any room of the house.

It is not hard to see on the horizon that you, the home inspector, will be asked to check out those "outlets," just as assuredly as you will be asked to check out the electrical outlets.

At that point, the options for you will be to say, "I don't know how to do that and I don't know anyone who does," "I have a partnership with a local home-technology integrator who can service the system (for a fee)," or, "Sure. I have learned how to do that."

Where to Learn

Although the home technology industry has thus far focused on new-home builders and the manufacturers and installers of equipment, more and more programs are being offered that home inspectors are eligible to take (for a fee) where they can learn about the latest innovations.

The Custom Electronic Design and Installation Association (CEDIA) holds an annual convention—the CEDIA Expo—where inspectors may learn more about how built-in systems work. The best place to see what CEDIA is up to: *www.CEDIA.net*.

During the CEDIA Expo, installers (and inspectors) may go through hands-on rigorous training sessions. In the end, those who take the course become certified installers (level 1 or level 2). More importantly, they gain understanding of how high-tech components are supposed to work.

Another great place to learn is the International Builders Show, sponsored by the National Association of Home Builders. The Tech Home Expo is part of the builders show, and again, rigorous training sessions are held for members who want to become more knowledgeable about the burgeoning number of high-tech add-ons going into the modern home.

The Computing Technology Industry Association, *comptia.org*, is yet another place for home inspectors to learn today what they may need to know tomorrow. Through CompTIA, inspectors may earn the HTI+ (home technology integrators) certification so they can troubleshoot automated home systems such as home security, audio/video, home computer networks, electrical wiring, HVAC, cable/satellite systems, broadband, and, of course, structured wiring.

Finally, there is also Electronic Home Expo (*ehexpo.com*) held twice annually—usually on either coast—where inspectors can attend multiday "boot camps" on installing and troubleshooting electronic systems. There also are more general classes at the Expo to learn about how systems are marketed and what they do.

Why Jump in Now?

What should spark your interest in the growing electronic home portion of the industry is that real estate agents know almost nothing about how systems work, and therefore are not able to market them to consumers.

Agents who list high-tech homes rarely take time to find out from homeowners how the systems operate. "Agents sell square feet and number of bedrooms," says Knott. "They usually tell the seller to negotiate for the electronic components outside of the deal." Agents who bring buyers through homes also usually don't realize, or even recognize, the value that structured wiring can bring.

A trained home inspector not only can recognize that value but also can explain to the homebuyer how to use the system, or explain if there are deficiencies in it.

"A growing number of homebuilders are installing whole-house computer systems with flat panel monitors in each room," says Knott. "But if the current homeowner doesn't explain the system to the new buyers, the full capabilities of the systems are not going to be passed along.

"These are the kinds of situations where a home inspector can add value to the inspection, either by knowing about the systems or partnering with a systems integrator who does."

Be warned, however, that with every new technology system comes expensive new hardware to test it with. Inspectors who provide ancillary services in monitoring high-tech systems will have to take their fees to a higher level as well.

CHAPTER 22

Why Do People Fail?

Every year a large number of people go into this business, and a large number are forced out. Why?

By some estimates, the turnover rate in this industry is a whopping 50 percent.

Think of it. Millions of homes are being inspected annually, and the number is steadily increasing. At the same time, demand is growing for other specialized varieties of inspections. Without question, this is an industry with lots of room to expand.

So why do half of the inspectors bail out?

It might have something to do with those ads portraying home inspection as a get-rich-quick business that's simple to start and easy to succeed at, with no limits on the number of inspections out there to put cash in your pockets.

But it goes beyond that, say both veterans and newcomers. They believe people fail for a variety of reasons, but all pretty much center on a failure to understand some fundamental truths.

Let's look at some of these.

Home Inspection is a Business

Bottom-line: This means you need a plan, you need money, and you need patience because the words *overnight success* are rare in any business.

"You have to build referrals, you have to build relationships," says Michael Casey of Haymarket, Virginia, who helps run inspection schools across the country. "You don't just put a number in the phone book and expect the phone to ring."

And Casey notes that getting from here to there takes time and money. For example, you need training ($3,000–$4,000), tools ($1,000–$1,500), and E&O insurance ($3,000).

"Including marketing materials, you should plan on $10,000 to $15,000 to get started, not including what you need to support yourself until profitable. Then it depends on what you put into it," he says.

Stan Garnet of Inspectors Associates Inc. in Atlanta is among the veteran inspectors who estimate it can take two to three years to really establish a strong home inspection business.

"You better have another job that's bringing money in, and if you don't have another job, you need to have enough to cover your living expenses," says Garnet. "Unless you have initial contacts and are extremely aggressive with good marketing skills, this is going to be a problem in the first year.

"Most of the guys who run through our classes have full-time jobs and are stepping into this and positioning themselves until they can leave their full-time jobs."

Garnet agrees that people often believe they can just jump into home inspection and do well.

Garnet cautions, "There's investment one needs to make with time and money."

You Can't Succeed Without Marketing

Going back to what was said above (and in Chapter 6), putting your number in the telephone book isn't going to make your phone ring. You have to sell yourself and your services.

> "The truth is that starting a home inspection business is like starting any other business. Just because you pass the test, just because you have all this background information, doesn't mean you don't still have to build your business. You have to build credibility. It's going to be a slow start unless you're already tied in—your wife or husband is a real estate agent, or you have friends or family to provide these leads." ∎

"I think a lack of marketing skills is the biggest problem," says Nick Gromicko, executive director of the National Association of Certified Home Inspectors. "They just don't have any concept that they have to market themselves. A lot of inspectors go out of business because they don't realize that marketing is half of the business."

Gromicko strongly feels that the marketing today must include the Internet, citing statistics that show the overwhelming number of homebuyers will go online first to look for a home and are used to doing their research on the World Wide Web.

You Need Good Communication Skills

As we've said in previous chapters, success requires that you not only be able to make your expertise known to the general public in order to line up business, you also need to be skilled in the best way to report on what you find during your inspection.

"Where the failing is, is that they're not good communicators," says Garnet. "It's really hard to find that all-around person that is a good communicator and a good marketer."

He says many times people don't understand why they can't make it in the home inspection business.

"When you sit and have a conversation with them, for some of us it's fairly obvious why they didn't succeed. It's not because they were not good home inspectors. It was because they could not relate to the people they had to deal with—the homebuyer and the real estate agent.

"That will knock you off the top pretty quickly."

Again, it is your job to objectively—and without emotion—report what you find and convey the significance of your findings in a manner that gives your client sufficient information to make a decision on what to do next. This can include asking the seller to remedy the problem, renegotiating the deal, or walking away altogether.

Education Is Important

Those who have been in this business for a while firmly believe you should have formal training before you launch your home inspection career and that you will need continuing education to prosper.

Although there are states that have just a few education requirements, or none at all, for someone to put out a shingle as a home inspector, expertise is needed in such a variety of areas that being an authority in all of them without formal training is difficult, if not impossible.

"They come in ill-prepared, without training—not having the ability to make good observations," says Ralph Wirth, a 20-year home inspector from Housing Consultants Inc. in Louisville, Kentucky. "They make mistakes and they are not financially able to handle them. The failure is not having the proper preparation to come into the industry."

Jay Schnoor of Professional Home Inspection Company Inc. in La Crescent, Minnesota, says inspectors who fail often "are not dedicated to the learning process."

"There are a lot of training mediums available. Each association has annual training opportunities. A lot of inspectors don't take part in those. The associations also have online forums where we can e-mail questions that came up during that day, or about something in general."

Schnoor believes those who do not take advantage of opportunities to continue to educate themselves "are not dedicated to their profession" and may very well be those who jumped in after reading ads promising them they could make $1,000 a day conducting home inspections.

Lynette Gebben of AmeriSpec in Madison, Wisconsin, says many people going into home inspection "don't really realize what it takes to be a good home inspector—both in the amount of time and the amount of dedication for continuing knowledge that it takes."

The Home Inspection Is Only a Part of the Job

Veteran inspectors agree that many newcomers don't understand that there's much more to the business than walking through a house and checking things, and even beyond selling yourself and communicating with others in the real estate transaction.

Inspectors are probably aware that a client wants a written report but again, the interaction can continue beyond that.

"Sometimes there are older part-timers who want a job that they can do a little bit a week and make some income," says Gebben. "They don't realize the inspection portion is only a portion of running a successful business. There are all the phone calls, questions from agents and lenders, and that's on top of the inspections. You often work through the day and throughout the weekend."

There Is Liability

When you are dealing with a big-ticket item such as a home, people expect you to not make mistakes while doing your general overview of the property. And even if you have convinced them that you can't see through walls or inside them, they may seek a legal remedy if something comes to light that they believe you should have found.

You'd be hard-pressed to find much about "liability" in those glossy ads urging you to become a home inspector.

"There is a lot of advertising on TV and in popular publications that makes it look like a very easy business to be a professional home inspector," says John Merritt of AmeriSpec in Santa Rosa, California.

"They take a correspondence course, but then there's the liability issue. There is a lot of liability in this business and a lot of inspectors don't carry professional insurance and they end up losing some of their assets."

While many inspectors believe that such insurance, including Errors and Omissions, is an essential tool in their arsenal, others fear that carrying it can make them a target for sue-happy disgruntled clients. And even if they win the case, the inspector loses time and energy in the process.

"I didn't have it for a number of years. The reason: I always felt I did my job properly and never had any lawsuits," says Dennis Robitaille of Able Home Inspection in Saugus, Massachusetts, whose state now requires E&O insurance for licensing.

"Once you have E&O, you're a target. After one year of licensing and mandatory E&O, I got my first lawsuit."

The lawsuit, he says, partially involved mold inside the walls. "I don't have X-ray vision. But the lawyer knows I've got E&O,'" said Robitaille.

Robitaille says even if he eventually wins the entire case, he fears E&O could be more difficult to obtain, and "the next year, my premiums could double in cost to around $5,000."

CHAPTER 23

In Conclusion . . .

Home inspecting can be both enjoyable and
lucrative. You'll like it here.

I n the end, it will be up to you to begin. Home inspection could be a terrific profession for you. Or it might not.

That's all up to you.

Hopefully, this book will make it a little easier for you to decide whether you are ready to "come on in" and join this profession.

There's no question that with every passing week, home inspection does become more of a profession. Licensing is spreading and no doubt will expand to all 50 states in one form or another. More continuing education is available. People expect more. Real estate agents will expect more. And the courts will expect more.

Nonetheless, you can do this.

Home inspection is a business that doesn't care about your gender, your race, your age, or your background.

It does want you to be interested in how things work. You need an eye for detail. You have to be able to communicate your findings in an unemotional, straightforward, and knowledgeable way.

As Bill Mason, a home inspector from Sarasota, Florida, defined the task: "Inspect, detect, and direct."

You'll also probably have to convince your client of that. There's no question that there's a huge misconception among members of the public about just how far a home inspection should go. That's one area where the home inspection industry needs to do better.

In the meantime, it often becomes part of the home inspector's job to explain the limits, says John Merritt of Santa Rosa, California.

"I don't think people really understand the limitations of an inspection. We're not supermen—we can't see into walls. We can't possibly inspect everything in a house," says Merritt.

"We try to explain that to people when we first meet them— that we can't get into inaccessible areas, that we can't see inside your walls. But we will do the best job we can based on what's visible and readily accessible."

Every national organization's standards of practice and state laws will back you up on that. But again, that doesn't mean you won't be questioned, and accused, about your X-ray vision or lack thereof.

There's no doubt that education is important in this business, both in terms of educating the public and yourself. Part of the movement to regulate home inspectors definitely involves just how educated you should be. Without question, we believe you should have formal training before you inspect your first house, whether you are required to or not. You can't get it from this book, but you can from a classroom or a computer. However, your real skills will come from doing.

"School would be like anything else. It's basic training," says Dennis Robitaille of Saugus, Massachusetts. "Anybody who goes to these so-called training courses and thinks they're going to come out and be a home inspector is wrong. They only get the rudimentary basics about inspecting. They're really just novices. They're going to develop their abilities as they begin working in the field."

You'll also need to continue educating yourself. States and organizations require it. But you also must have it to protect your clients—and yourself. There are online opportunities to practice inspections and gain continuing education. There are also workshops and conferences. And you can also learn from your peers on a regular basis through home inspector organizations and the Internet.

One of the most fascinating things about this business involves what seems to be two opposing truths:

1. All houses are pretty much built the same.
2. No two houses are alike.

That definitely keeps things interesting. But it also can make things difficult. That's why continuing to educate yourself is so important.

True, it will take time and it will take money. But so does succeeding in this or any other business.

You won't find success overnight. It will be up to you to figure out the shortest route from here to there. By doing a good job, you will get more business. But unless you're independently wealthy, there's no doubt that marketing is going to be important too.

There are varying viewpoints on how long it will take for you to make a living at this. Again, it depends on how hard you want to work and how good a living you need to make. But some experts believe that if you can last in this business for 18 months, you're probably going to make it—although it may take two to three years to establish yourself at the level you'd prefer.

One thing is for sure: success in home inspection—and most everything else—results from a three-part process:

1. Devise a plan.
2. Move forward.
3. Do it now.

Of all three, "Do it now" is by far the most important.

A good plan without action can only fail. A bad plan with enough work often succeeds. If you want to be a success, you need to put *you* in motion.

With the home inspection industry steadily evolving into a more generally accepted "profession," its presence is going to be requested in more and more of the millions of real estate transactions every year.

There is no better time to be in home inspection.

Do it now.

Here is a list of some common terms used in the home inspection industry. Some home inspector associations also have glossaries available on their Web sites.

A/C An abbreviation for air conditioner or air-conditioning.

accessible Can be approached or entered by the inspector safely, without difficulty, fear, or danger.

access panel An opening in the wall or ceiling near the fixture that allows access for servicing the plumbing/electrical system.

activate To use normal control means to turn on, supply power, or enable systems or devices.

agent Someone who represents a consumer in a real estate deal. That consumer may be either the buyer or the seller. An agent is someone who will look after the interests of the consumer. Note: Despite popular use, the terms *agent, broker,* and *REALTOR*® do not all mean the same thing. *See* broker; REALTOR®.

agreement A legally binding contract between two or more persons.

air duct These are usually made of sheet metal, and carry cooled or heated air to all rooms.

alarm system Warning devices, installed or freestanding, that include but are not limited to smoke alarms; carbon monoxide detectors, flue gas and other spillage detectors; security equipment, and ejector pumps.

aluminum wire A conductor made of aluminum for carrying electricity.

American Society of Home Inspectors (ASHI) The American Society of Home Inspectors is one of the largest and most generally known of the home inspector organizations. It is based in Des Plaines, Illinois. Some states use its Code of Ethics as their own.

amperage The rate of flow of electricity through wire—measured in terms of amperes.

amps (amperes) The rate at which electricity flows through a conductor.

ancillary inspection services These are offered in addition to the traditional home inspection. These may include environmental testing or looking for wood-destroying pests.

appliance A household device operated by electricity or gas. Does not include central heating, central cooling, or plumbing components.

appraisal A report from an independent person estimating value of real estate.

asbestos A common form of magnesium silicate used in various construction products to make them more stable or fire-resistant, but can cause lung cancer if its tiny fibers become airborne and are inhaled into the lungs.

associate member Beginning level of inspection association membership.

attic access An opening that is placed in the drywalled ceiling of a home providing access to the attic.

backflow Movement of water (or other liquid) in any direction other than that intended.

beam A supporting member either of wood or steel. Structural support member (steel, concrete, lumber) transversely supporting a load that transfers weight from one location to another.

below grade The portion of a building that is below ground level.

breaker box A metal box that contains circuit breakers or fuses that control the electrical current in a home.

breaker panel The electrical box that distributes electric power entering the home to each branch circuit (each plug and switch) and is comprised of circuit breakers.

broker A broker is someone who has received additional state-required training so that she or he may act as a supervisor over real estate sales agents.

BTU A measure of the capacity of a heating or cooling system. Abbreviation of British Thermal Unit. The amount of heat energy required to raise the temperature of one pound of water through a change of one degree Fahrenheit.

building code Minimum local or state regulations established to protect health and safety. They apply to building design, construction, rehabilitation, repair, materials, occupancy, and use. Community ordinances governing the manner in which a home may be constructed or modified.

building permit Written authorization from the city, county, or other governing regulatory body to construct or renovate a building.

buyer's agent A buyer's agent is legally obligated to represent the best interests of his or her client, the buyer.

candidate Beginning level of inspection association membership. *See* associate member.

carbon monoxide A colorless, odorless, highly poisonous gas formed by the incomplete combustion of carbon.

ceiling joist One of a series of parallel framing members used to support ceiling loads and supported in turn by larger beams, girders, or bearing walls. Also called *roof joists*.

ceramic tile A man-made or machine-made clay tile used to finish a floor or wall.

certification Generally speaking, a certification comes as a result of training that helps someone function in a number of different areas. It differs from a designation, which usually covers training in one specific discipline.

chapter A local group or branch of members of a larger association.

circuit A network of wiring that typically commences at a panel box, feeds electricity to outlets, and ultimately returns to the panel box.

circuit breaker A protective device that automatically opens an electrical circuit when it is overloaded.

client Someone who has entered into an agreement with a home inspector and agreed to terms of compensation for work by the inspector.

closing (settlement) The meeting of all parties or their representatives in the final transfer of property to a new owner.

closing costs Various tangent expenses involved in a real estate closing that are separate from the actual cost of the property.

Code of Ethics A document provided by members of an organization that states how those members should work with clients, customers, and each other as either colleagues or competitors.

commission In real estate, this is a percentage of a sales contract that goes to a real estate brokerage for selling a home. Typical commission rates are from 4.5 percent to 7 percent. (A 6 percent commission on $100,000 would be $6,000.) They are not set by law.

component A component is a permanently installed or attached fixture, element, or part of a system.

condensation Water condensing on walls, ceilings, and pipes. Normal in areas of high humidity, usually controlled by ventilation or a dehumidifier.

condition The visible and conspicuous state of being of an object.

Conditions, Covenants, and Restrictions (CC&R)   The rules that homeowners agree to abide by when moving into a community governed by a neighborhood association or condo board.

condominium (also **condo**) A system of real estate ownership where there is separate ownership of units in a multiunit project, with each separate unit ownership being coupled with an undivided share in the entire project less all of the units.

conduit A hollow pipe casing through which electric lines run.

continuing education Ongoing education, obtained through courses or workshops, that often is a requirement for state licensing or membership in a home inspection association. CE usually involves attending certain specified classes, earning a specific number of credit hours over a specific number of years in order to keep a license or membership active.

contract or sale Agreement by one party to buy and another party to sell a piece of property for a specific price.

contractor An individual licensed to perform certain types of construction activities.

cooperative (apartment) An incorporated apartment building in which the tenants each own shares of the building, which entitles them to live in the building and make decisions regarding the building as a whole.

corrosion The deterioration of metal by chemical or electrochemical reaction resulting from exposure to weathering, moisture, chemicals, or other agents or media.

crawlspace A shallow open area between the ground and the lowest floor structural component that is normally enclosed by the foundation wall.

decorative Ornamental; not required for the operation of the essential systems and components of a home.

describe To report a system or component by its type or other observed significant characteristics to distinguish it from other systems or components.

designation Generally, a designation is awarded after education is completed in a single discipline.

detrimental conditions Conditions that an inspector believes may be unsafe, unhealthy, or otherwise harmful to the inspector or to the property.

disclosures Items that, by law, must be revealed by buyers, sellers, real estate agents, lenders, and others. Sellers, for instance, must reveal certain problems, such as leaky roofs, to homebuyers.

dismantle To take apart or remove any component, device, or piece of equipment that would not be taken apart or removed by a homeowner in the course of normal and routine maintenance.

EIFS (Exterior Insulation Finish System) Also known as *synthetic stucco*, EIFS is designed to keep water out and energy in. If water seeps inside, however, it can become trapped and rot the wood underneath.

EMF (Electric and magnetic fields) Invisible lines of force that surround any electrical device. Power lines, electrical wiring, and electrical equipment produce EMF. Some laboratory studies have reported EMF exposure can produce biological effects, including changes in functions of cells and tissues.

engineering service Any professional service or creative work requiring engineering education, training and experience, and the application of special knowledge of the mathematical, physical, and engineering sciences to such professional service or creative work as consultation, investigation, evaluation, planning, design, and supervision of construction for the purpose of assuring compliance with the specifications and design, in conjunction with structures, buildings, machines, equipment, works, or processes.

Errors and Omissions (E&O) insurance Insurance coverage for things that go wrong after the fact. May cover liability and legal costs.

evaluate To form an opinion of or judge an item or condition.

exclusive buyer's agent Someone who works only with homebuyers and does not list homes at any time.

Federal Housing Administration (FHA) A federal agency that insures first mortgages, enabling lenders to lend a very high percentage of the sales price.

fee for service The concept that a real estate agent should be paid whether or not a deal closes. Agents may charge an hourly rate, or make a la carte charges on such things as holding an open house.

fixtures Personal property that is attached to real property, such as chandeliers, window blinds, and medicine cabinets.

formaldehyde Widely used in the manufacture of building materials and household products, formaldehyde also can be emitted by unvented fuel-burning appliances. The gas can cause respiratory problems, and possibly cancer.

for sale by owner (FSBO) Properties whose owners are attempting to sell them without assistance from a real estate professional.

foundation The base upon which a wall or structure sits. Usually made of masonry, concrete, or stone, a foundation normally is partially underground.

function The action for which an item, component, or system is used or fitted.

functional The ability to perform a function.

functional drainage If a supply faucet is left on, a drain empties in a reasonable amount of time without overflowing.

functional flow Enough flow of water to provide an uninterrupted supply to the faucet farthest from the source when a single intermediate, unrestricted tap is operated at the same time.

further evaluation Examination and analysis by a qualified professional, tradesman, or service technician beyond what a home inspector provides.

habitable Suitable for humans to live there.

habitable spaces Rooms used for sleeping, sitting, bathing, eating, cooking, or with toilets. However, closets, halls, storage spaces, and utility areas are not usually considered habitable spaces.

heat source Something from which heat is intended to be emitted, such as radiators, heat pipe, ductwork, and so forth.

home inspection The process by which an inspector visually examines and evaluates the readily accessible systems and components of a house.

homeowner Someone who has title to a property and is legally entitled to sell it.

household appliances Installed or free-standing kitchen, laundry, and similar appliances.

homeowners insurance Real estate insurance protecting against loss caused by fire, some natural causes, vandalism, and so forth, depending on the terms of the policy. Also includes coverage such as personal liability and theft away from home.

HUD The U.S. Department of Housing and Urban Development, which is involved in many facets of the real estate industry.

inspect To examine readily accessible systems and components of a building.

inspector A person hired to examine systems or components of a building. Not all inspectors are licensed, and in some states, special training is not even required.

installed Attached so that removal requires tools.

intended function The ability of an item to perform the usual function for which it was designed, and in a condition appropriate for the function, age, and location.

judgment The determination of a court regarding the rights of parties in an action.

lawyer, real estate Not all lawyers are the same. "Real estate attorneys" are often hired to review real estate contracts.

lead-based paint Although lead in paint has been outlawed since 1978, it can be found in older homes and is a hazard only if it is peeling, chipping, or cracking.

lender A lender is a bank or company (or even an individual) that actually risks its money in making a loan. *See also* mortgage broker.

license A state- or local-granted permit given to home inspectors to evaluate a property for compensation.

listing A listing is a house for sale by a real estate agent. When the owner of the home agrees to allow an agent to sell it, the owner will sign a "listing agreement," a contract outlining what the agent will do to market the home in exchange for a fee of a certain amount.

listing agent A listing agent is the agent who has a signed agreement with the person selling the house. *See also* selling agent.

mentor Someone who explains policies and procedures, as well as demonstrates skills to a new inspector.

mold and mildew Fungi that grow on surfaces when relative humidity is high and can result in health problems inside a house.

mortgage A pledge of property to a creditor as security for the payment of a debt.

mortgage broker A mortgage broker is someone who helps homebuyers sort through loan packages offered by various lenders. *See also* lender.

National Association of Certified Home Inspectors (NACHI)   The National Association of Certified Home Inspectors claims to be the largest home inspector organization. It offers various online tools and owns numerous inspector-related Web sites. It is based in Valley Forge, Pennsylvania.

National Association of Home Inspectors (NAHI) One of the older home inspector groups, the National Association of Home Inspectors calls itself the "inspector-friendly" group. Based in Minneapolis, NAHI's Code of Ethics and test are used by some states in their regulations.

National Association of REALTORS® (NAR) The National Association of REALTORS® is a trade association of real estate agents. The

NAR owns the word *REALTOR*® and prohibits its use by real estate licensees who are not members of the trade organization. It has a very active political lobby in Washington, D.C., and state legislatures around the country to help lawmakers define business dealings between real estate license holders and other industries.

normal operating controls Devices such as thermostats, switches, or valves intended to be operated to control systems and components.

open house A home for sale held open for public visitation by either the listing agent or an assistant for a specific number of hours.

operate To cause activated equipment or systems to perform their intended function(s).

polybutylene (PB) plumbing Commonly installed in mobile homes and apartments through the 1980s, PB plumbing was the subject of a class action lawsuit because of leaking.

radon An odorless, invisible, and radioactive gas formed by the natural breakdown of uranium in soil, rock, and water, and that seeps into homes. It is believed to be the second leading cause of lung cancer.

readily accessible Available for visual inspection without requiring the moving of personal property, dismantling, destructive measures, or any action likely to involve risk to property or people.

real estate Land and anything permanently affixed to the land, such as buildings, fences, and other things attached to the buildings, such as plumbing and heating fixtures or other such items that would be personal property if not attached.

REALTOR® A REALTOR® is a member of the National Association of REALTORS®, a trade association that acts on behalf of the nation's real estate sales force. Membership is voluntary. Only those who are members of the group may call themselves REALTORS®.

recreational facilities These are normally outside the scope of a general home inspection and include spas, saunas, steam baths, swimming pools, and exercise, entertainment, athletic, playground, or other similar equipment and associated accessories.

referral fee Money either paid or received in the transfer of business from one person or company to another.

representative number Enough components to serve as a typical, or characteristic, example of the item or items inspected.

roof drainage systems Components used to carry water off a roof and away from a building.

sales associate A real estate license holder. The entry-level position for most agents.

selling agent The real estate agent who brings the buyer to the deal typically is called the *selling agent*. Under certain circumstances, the selling agent also may be the *buyer's agent.*

settlement (closing) The meeting of all parties or their representatives in the final transfer of property to a new owner.

shut down In terms of an inspection, this is a condition in which a system or component cannot be operated by normal operating controls.

significantly deficient Unsafe or not functioning.

slab on grade These are structures without a crawlspace that are in direct contact with the soil.

solid-fuel-burning appliances A hearth and fire chamber or similar prepared place in which a fire may be built and which is built in conjunction with a chimney; or a listed assembly of a fire chamber, its chimney, and related factory-made parts designed for assembly without requiring field construction.

Standards of Practice The minimum guidelines for conducting a home inspection, as established by a group or state. The standards outline the various components and procedures, scope, and the limitations.

structural component A component that supports nonvariable forces or weights (dead loads) and variable forces or weights (live loads).

synthetic stucco This exterior insulation finishing system, also known as EIFS, is designed to keep water out and energy in. If water seeps inside, however, it can become trapped and rot the wood underneath.

system A combination of interacting or interdependent components, which together carry out one or more functions.

technically exhaustive An investigation that involves dismantling, or extensive use of advanced techniques, measurements, instruments, testing, calculations, or other means.

title A combination of all of the elements that constitute the highest level right to own, possess, use, control, enjoy, and dispose of real estate or an inheritable right or interest therein.

title insurance Required by most lenders before a mortgage can be approved, title insurance guarantees that the property is free of claims from unknown third parties, such as former spouses or workers.

underfloor crawlspace The area within the confines of the foundation and between the ground and the underside of the floor.

unsafe A condition in a readily accessible, installed system or component that is judged to pose a significant risk of personal injury during normal day-to-day use. It can be caused by damage, deterioration, improper installation, or a change in accepted residential construction standards.

verify To confirm or substantiate something.

wiring methods Identification of electrical conductors or wires by their general type, such as "nonmetallic sheathed cable" (Romex).

A

AAHI. *See* American Association of Home Inspectors
AAMC. *See* Accredited Association Management Company
ABR. *See* Accredited Buyer Representative
ABRM. *See* Accredited Buyer Representative Manager
Accredited Association Management Company (AAMC), 75
Accredited Buyer Representative (ABR), 74, 75
Accredited Buyer Representative Manager (ABRM), 75
Accredited Residential Originator (ARO), 78–79
Accredited Residential Underwriter (ARU), 79
Accuracy, 122
Adult education, 47-48
Adverse conditions, 16
Advertising, 43
AHWD. *See* At Home with Diversity
AII. *See* American Institute of Inspectors
AII Certified Member, 50
AIS. *See* American Inspectors Society
American Association of Home Inspectors (AAHI), 50
American Inspectors Society (AIS), 50, 156–57
American Institute of Inspectors (AII), 50, 156
American Society of Home Inspectors (ASHI)
　ethics, 141, 142–44
　origins, 130
　overview, 150–51
　member benefits, 151
　membership levels, 50
　training, 20
AMS. *See* Association Management Specialist
Ancillary services, 177–83
Anderson, Mallory, 91, 99
Answering machine, 43
Appliances, 7
Appraisal, 12, 167
Appraiser, 71–72, 78
Apprentice, 23
Arc fault, 39
ARO. *See* Accredited Residential Originator
ARU. *See* Accredited Residential Underwriter
Asbestos, 170, 179
ASHI. *See* American Society of Home Inspectors
As is, 134
Association Management Specialist (AMS), 75
At Home with Diversity (AHWD), 75
Attic, 27–28

B

Background, 5
Balance, 122
Barroner, Shelly, 35–36, 94
Binoculars, 38
Bloxom, Troy, 94
Bond, 42
Brochures, 57–58
Broker liability, 131
Building products, 173–74
Building systems, 19
　electrical, 26
　exterior, 24
　heating and cooling, 26–27
　insulating and ventilating, 27–28

interior, 29–30
plumbing, 28–29
roofing, 25–26
structural, 24–25
Business
basics, 58
card, 49, 53, 73–74
insurance, 42
phone, 43
plan, 10
Buyer
agenda, 81–82
keeper list, 69–70
on location, 118–20
questions, 116–20
safety, 120–21
Buyer agent, 67, 82

C

Cabinets, 29
Carbon monoxide (CO), 39, 170–71, 180
Carson, Alan, 86–87, 134–35, 140–41
Casey, Michael, 15, 21, 99–100, 192
CCIM. *See* Certified Commercial Investment Member
C-CREC. *See* Certified-Consumer Real Estate Consultant
CEBA. *See* Certified Exclusive Buyer Agent
CEDIA. *See* Custom Electronic Design and Installation Association
CEDIA Expo, 188
Ceiling, 25, 29
Cell phone, 43, 53
Certification
definition of, 73
reason for, 74
sampling, 75–79
Certified Commercial Investment Member (CCIM), 74, 75
Certified-Consumer Real Estate Consultant (C-CREC), 75

Certified Exclusive Buyer Agent (CEBA), 76
Certified Graduate Associate (CGA), 76
Certified Graduate Builder (CGB), 76
Certified Home Inspector (CHI), 50, 155
Certified Luxury Home Marketing Specialist (CLHMS), 76
Certified Mortgage Banker (CMB), 79
Certified Mortgage Consultant (CMC), 79
Certified Mortgage Technologist (CMT), 79
Certified New Home Marketing Professional (CMP), 76
Certified New Home Sales Professional (CSP), 77
Certified Property Manager (CPM), 76
Certified Real Estate Appraiser (CREA), 78
Certified Real Estate Brokerage Manager (CRB), 76
Certified Real Estate Inspector (CRI), 50, 148, 152
Certified Relocation Professional (CRP), 77
Certified Residential Mortgage Specialist (CRMS), 79
Certified Residential Specialist (CRS), 74, 77
CGA. *See* Certified Graduate Associate
CGB. *See* Certified Graduate Builder
Challenges, 7
CHI. *See* Certified Home Inspector
CIRMS. *See* Community Insurance and Risk Management Specialist
CLHMS. *See* Certified Luxury Home Marketing Specialist
Client, 6, 81–82, 86–88
Clissold, Mardi, 32, 149
CMB. *See* Certified Mortgage Banker

CMC. *See* Certified Mortgage Consultant
CMP. *See* Certified New Home Marketing Professional
CMT. *See* Certified Mortgage Technologist
CO. *See* Carbon monoxide
Commercial building inspection, 182
Communication skills, 15, 193–94
Community Insurance and Risk Management Specialist (CIRMS), 76
Company name, 48
Competition, 6
CompTIA, 188
Computer, 42
Computer tablets, 42–43
Computing Technology Industry Association, 188
Construction methods, 173
Consumer activist movement, 130
Consumer Home Inspection Hotline, 153
Consumer Product Safety Commission, 105
Contingency clause, 70, 73
Continuing education, 44, 194–95, 198–99
Contracts, 3
Correspondence courses, 22–23
Counselor of Real Estate (CRE), 76
Counteroffer, 70
Countertops, 29
Court system, 6
CPM. *See* Certified Property Manager
Crawlspace, 27–28, 112
CRB. *See* Certified Real Estate Brokerage Manager
CRE. *See* Counselor of Real Estate
CREA. *See* Certified Real Estate Appraiser
CRI. *See* Certified Real Estate Inspector
CRMS. *See* Certified Residential Mortgage Specialist

CRP. *See* Certified Relocation Professional
CRS. *See* Certified Residential Specialist
CSP. *See* Certified New Home Sales Professional
Custom Electronic Design and Installation Association (CEDIA), 188
Customer service, 14–16

D

Dangers, 109–13
Deductive reasoning skills, 21
Designation
    definition of, 74
    reasons for, 74
    sampling, 75–79
Devices, electrical, 26
Digital camera, 38–39
Disaster, 182
Disclosure issues, 106–7
Discount coupon, 60–61, 63
Distinguished Real Estate Instructor (DREI), 77
Domain name, 55
Doors, 24, 29
Drain, 28
Drainage, 24, 25
Drainage sumps, 29
DREI. *See* Distinguished Real Estate Instructor

E

Easton v. Strassburger, 129, 131–33
Education, 194–95
EIFS. *See* Exterior insulation and finish system
800 number, 49
Electrical circuit analyzer, 39
Electrical systems, 26
Electric and magnetic field (EMF), 171
Electronic Home Expo, 188–89

Electronic Real Estate Professional
(e-PRO), 77
E-mail, 42
  address, 53–55
  attachments, 54
  automatic response, 54
  signature, 54
EMF. *See* Electric and magnetic
  field
Energy efficiency analysis, 182
Engineering report, 12
Environmental inspection, 179–81
e-PRO. *See* Electronic Real Estate
  Professional
Equipment, electrical, 26
Errors and omissions insurance
  cost of, 5, 42, 196
  perceptions, 134–35
  state requirements, 137
Ethics, 7, 119–20, 139–45
Expertise, 14
Expert witness, 182–83
Exterior insulation and finish sys-
  tem (EIFS), 172–73, 180
Exterior systems, 24

F

Facilitator, 68
Failure rate, 7
Fast Track, 163–64
Fax machine, 43
Federal Emergency Management
  Agency (FEMA), 182
Federal Housing Administration,
  174
Federal regulation, 166–67
Fee-for-service agent, 68
Fees, 3
  NACHI recommendations, 95–
    96
  payment of, 96
  professional organization, 147
  researching, 91–96
  setting, 89–91
FEMA. *See* Federal Emergency Man-
  agement Agency

FIHI. *See* Foundation for Indepen-
  dent Home Inspection
Financial plan, 10–11
Fireplace, 29–30
Fixtures, 26, 28
Flashing, roof, 25
Flashlight, 39
Floor, 24–25, 29
Formaldehyde, 171
Foundation, 24
Foundation for Independent Home
  Inspection (FIHI), 51, 159
Franchise, 11, 22, 46
French, Bill, 121
Fuel distribution system, 28
Fuel storage, 28

G

GAA. *See* General Accredited
  Appraiser
Garage door, 29
Garnet, Stan, 16–17, 92, 192, 193
Gas leak detector, 39
Gebben, Lynette, 15–16, 101, 195
Gender, 5, 31–36
General Accredited Appraiser
  (GAA), 78
Gladstone, Stephen, 21–22, 92–93,
  178–79
GMB. *See* Graduate Master Builder
Grading, 24
Graduate Master Builder (GMB), 77
Graduate-REALTOR® Institute (GRI),
  77
GRI. *See* Graduate-REALTOR® Insti-
  tute
Gromicko, Nick, 105, 149–50, 193
Ground fault circuit tester, 39

H

Hazardous issues, 169–73
HBIA. *See* Historic Building Inspec-
  tors Association
Heating and cooling systems, 26–27

Hickson, Alyssa, 33–34, 62, 93–94, 122
HIF. *See* Housing Inspection Foundation
High-tech gadgets, 185–89
Historic Building Inspectors Association (HBIA), 51, 157–58
Home Builders' Research Center, 174
Home checkup/maintenance, 182
Home inspection. *See* Inspection
Homeowners, marketing to, 64
Home technology integrator (HTI+), 188
Home warranty, 182
Housing Inspection Foundation (HIF), 50, 51, 154–55
HTI+. *See* Home technology integrator

I

IHINA. *See* Independent Home Inspectors of North America
Incentive bonus, 165
Independent Home Inspectors of North America (IHINA), 51, 158
Independent owner, 11
Inspection
    depth of, 103–7
    do-it-yourself, 123–28
    explanation of, 12–14
    limits, 198
    mirror, 39
    report, 61–62, 98
    time, 98
Insulating and ventilating systems, 27–28
Insurance inspection, 182
Interior systems, 27–28, 29–30
International Builders Show, 188
Internet, 42, 149–50

K

Keeper list, 69–70
Kickbacks, 165

Knott, Jason, 187, 189
Knowledge areas, 20
Known defects, 134

L

Ladder, 39–40, 110–12
Lead-based paint, 171–72, 180
Leadership Training Graduate (LTG), 77
Legal fees, 5
Lender, 69, 78–79
Level, 40
Liability, 124–25, 133–36, 196
License, 42
Lingsch v. Savage, 130
Listing agent, 67–68, 82
Litigation, 14
LTG. *See* Leadership Training Graduate

M

Mallet, 40
Marketing, 6
    basic tools, 48–62
    franchise, 46
    to homeowners, 64
    importance of, 193
    to mortgage bankers, 64
    to real estate agents, 62–63
    to real estate attorneys, 64
    referrals, 46–47
    to sellers, 64
    techniques, 47
    traditional, 45
Marotz, Diane, 32–33, 34, 48
Mason, Bill, 104–6, 197
Master Certified New Home Sales Professional (MCSP), 77
MCSP. *See* Master Certified New Home Sales Professional
Medical insurance, 42
Memberships, 44
Merritt, John, 16, 99, 195–96, 198
Moisture management, 27
Moisture meter, 40

Mold/mildew, 172, 180
Mooney, Alan, 126–28
Mortgage banker, 64, 69
Mortgage broker, 69
Motto, 49
Municipal inspector, 12

N

NABIE. *See* National Academy of
  Building Inspection Engineers
NACHI. *See* National Association of
  Certified Home Inspectors
NAHI. *See* National Association of
  Home Inspectors
NARIES. *See* National Association
  of Real Estate Inspection & Evalu-
  ation Services
National Academy of Building
  Inspection Engineers (NABIE),
  51, 154
National Association of Certified
  Home Inspectors (NACHI)
    ethics, 141, 142–44
    Internet opportunities, 149–50
    overview, 153–54
    membership levels, 51, 153
    recommendations, 95–96
National Association of Home
  Builders, 188
National Association of Home
  Inspectors (NAHI)
    certifications, 148
    ethics, 141, 142–44
    overview, 152–53
    member benefits, 152
    membership levels, 51, 152
National Association of Real Estate
  Inspection & Evaluation Services
  (NARIES), 51, 157
National Center for Healthy Hous-
  ing, 174
National Home Inspectors Examina-
  tion (NHIE)
    areas of knowledge, 20–21
    categories covered, 24–30
    cost, 21

National Institute of Building
  Inspectors (NIBI), 52, 155–56
Negligent referral, 85
New construction inspection, 182
Newsletters, 47
NHIE. *See* National Home Inspec-
  tors Examination
NIBI. *See* National Institute of
  Building Inspectors
NIBI Certified Inspector, 52
Norman, Don, 5, 92

O

Offer, 70
Open house, 47
Overhead, 44, 92–93

P

Pager, 43
Paintbrush, 40
Partnership for Response and
  Recovery, 182
PB. *See* Polybutylene plumbing
PCAM. *See* Professional Commu-
  nity Association Manager
Personality, 14–16
Pest inspection, 181
Physical limits, 98
Pictures, 58–59
Plumbing systems, 28–29
Pocket knife, 40
Poliferno, Frank, 100–101
Politics, 7, 161–67
Polybutylene (PB) plumbing, 172
Prelisting inspection, 48, 63, 88, 181
Prequalification letter, 69
Prices, 6, 60–61
Printer, 42
Product liability, 130
Product recalls, 105
Professional Community Associa-
  tion Manager (PCAM), 77
Professional insurance. *See* Errors
  and omissions insurance
Professionalism, 9–10, 42–44

Professional organizations, 147–59

Q

QSC. *See* Quality Service Certified
Qualifications, 59
Quality Service Certified (QSC), 78

R

RAA. *See* Residential Accredited
  Appraiser
Radon, 172, 180–81
Rate. *See* Prices
Real estate agent
  designations, 74–78
  marketing to, 62–63
  referrals, 84–86, 144–45
  types of, 67–68
Real estate attorney, 64, 72
Real estate transaction, 6, 13
  agent role, 67–68
  appraiser's role, 71–72
  counteroffer, 70
  inspector's role, 65–66
  mortgage banker role, 69
  mortgage lender role, 69
  offer, 70
  timeline, 66–67, 69–73, 82–84
  title company role, 72
Real Estate Buyer's Agent Council,
  75
Reciprocity, 165
Recommendations, 143
Referral, 46–47, 84–86
Referral fees, 143
Registered Home Inspector (RHI),
  52, 155
Regulations, 13–14
Reinspection fee, 91
Research, 22
Residential Accredited Appraiser
  (RAA), 78
RHI. *See* Registered Home Inspec-
  tor
Risk, 6
Robitaille, Dennis, 47, 94, 196, 198

Roof certification, 174
Roofing systems, 25–26, 27–28
Rosenthal, Harry, 136, 137
Ruhs, Janice, 15, 32, 36

S

Sales presentation, 63
Scheduling, 97–101
Schnoor, Jay, 15, 148, 149, 194
Screwdriver, 40–41
Seller
  agenda, 82
  as client, 87–88
  marketing to, 64
Seminars, 48
Senior Real Estate Specialist
  (SRES), 78
Senses, 20
Sensor pen, 39
Septic inspection, 181
Service panel, 26
Services, 60
Sewage ejection pumps, 29
Shirt, 61
Shoes, 41
Single component inspection, 181
SIOR. *See* Society of Industrial and
  Office REALTORS®
Skills, 3, 5
Skylights, 26
Slogan, 49
Society of Industrial and Office
  REALTORS® (SIOR), 78
Society of Professional Real Estate
  Inspectors (SPREI), 52
Software, 42
Special investigations, 183
SPREI. *See* Society of Professional
  Real Estate Inspectors
SRES. *See* Senior Real Estate Special-
  ist
Standards of practice, 14, 104
Start-up costs, 192
State regulation, 162–64
St. Louis, Kimberly, 33, 93
Structural systems, 24–25

Structured wiring, 187–88
Sump pumps, 29
Support groups, 7
Swimming pool/spa inspection, 181
Synergy, 165
Synthetic stucco, 172–73, 180

T

Tape measure, 41
Teague, Michelle, 31, 35, 93
Tech Home Expo, 188
Technical exam, 20
Telephone answering machine, 52
Termite inspection, 181
Testimonials, 59
Thermal insulation, 27
Thermometer, 41
Time investment, 199
Time management, 6
Title company, 72
Toolbox, 41
Tools, 5, 37–42
Trade associations, 165–66
Training, 20, 22–23, 198
Transaction broker, 68
Travel time, 97–98

Turnover rate, 191–96

U

UF. *See* Urea-formaldehyde
Urea-formaldehyde (UF), 171

V

Vegetation, 24
Vehicle, 41–42, 61
Ventilation system, 27–28
Vertical support structures, 25
Voice mail, 52

W

Walls, 24, 25, 29
Waste, 28
Water heating systems, 28
Water pressure meter, 42
Water quality testing, 181
Water supply distribution system, 28
Web site, 42, 55–57
Well inspection, 181
Windows, 24, 29
Wiring systems, 26
Wirth, Ralph, 101, 150, 194
Wood, Samuel, 71